PRIMER ON SOCIAL BONDS AND RECENT DEVELOPMENTS IN ASIA

FEBRUARY 2021

ASIAN DEVELOPMENT BANK

ADB

© 2021 Asian Development Bank
6 ADB Avenue, Mandaluyong City, 1550 Metro Manila, Philippines
Tel +63 2 8632 4444; Fax +63 2 8636 2444
www.adb.org

Some rights reserved. Published in 2021.

ISBN 978-92-9262-712-6 (print), 978-92-9262-713-3 (electronic), 978-92-9262-714-0 (ebook)
Publication Stock No. SPR210045-2
DOI: http://dx.doi.org/10.22617/SPR210045-2

The views expressed in this publication are those of the authors and do not necessarily reflect the views and policies of the Asian Development Bank (ADB) or its Board of Governors or the governments they represent.

ADB does not guarantee the accuracy of the data included in this publication and accepts no responsibility for any consequence of their use. The mention of specific companies or products of manufacturers does not imply that they are endorsed or recommended by ADB in preference to others of a similar nature that are not mentioned.

By making any designation of or reference to a particular territory or geographic area, or by using the term "country" in this document, ADB does not intend to make any judgments as to the legal or other status of any territory or area.

Corrigenda to ADB publications may be found at http://www.adb.org/publications/corrigenda.

Notes:
In this publication, "$" refers to United States dollars.
ADB recognizes "China" as the People's Republic of China; "Hong Kong" as Hong Kong, China; "Korea" as the Republic of Korea; "Taipei" as Taipei,China; and "Macau" as Macau, China.

Cover design by Francis Manio.

Contents

Tables, Figures, and Boxes

Foreword

The Asian Development Bank (ADB) is working closely with developing member economies to tackle the coronavirus disease (COVID-19) and mitigate its impact on developing Asia. The pandemic has had a pronounced effect on the region's economy, which is expected to contract on an annual basis for the first time in 6 decades. The downturn poses especially serious challenges to vulnerable groups. While developing Asian governments have introduced stimulus packages to support vulnerable groups, more resources can be mobilized via capital markets to support an inclusive recovery. Social bonds raise proceeds for projects with positive social outcomes and serve as a valuable financial instrument in this context.

The outbreak of COVID-19 has energized social bond financing both globally and in Asia, as evidenced by a rapid increase in social bond issuance. Nevertheless, compared to green bonds, the social bond market is still in a nascent stage of development. This study is the first comprehensive review of the various financial instruments that address social needs, with a focus on developing Asia's social bond markets. This report was produced under an ADB technical assistance program that promotes knowledge about financing investments with positive social impacts, raises awareness and interest in social bonds, and ultimately contributes to the development of social bond markets in Asia.

We are delighted to share the latest findings of the report, which analyzes the taxonomy of social investments and existing market practices, and presents the current profile of global and regional social bond markets. In addition, the report examines the social bond market from the market participant perspective, highlighting how social bonds channel private sector capital to investments with positive social externalities. The report makes it clear that social bond market development is vital for financing Asia's sustainable economic recovery from COVID-19. The report also outlines key barriers to market development and some potential solutions for overcoming them. Overall, social bonds can help the region meet its long-term Sustainable Development Goals and transition to a more inclusive recovery that benefits all Asians.

The study was prepared by Jane Hughes and Jason Mortimer under the direction of a team in ADB's Economic Research and Regional Cooperation Department, led by Shu Tian and supported by Donghyun Park, Kosintr Puongsophol, and Satoru Yamadera. Additional assistance and logistics support were provided by Mai Lin Villaruel and Rhia Theresa Bautista-Piamonte. Ulrich Volz served as reviewer and provided helpful comments. The authors are grateful to the many government officials and market participants who shared their views, experiences, and insights at the report's online workshop held on 8 October 2020.

Yasuyuki Sawada
Chief Economist and Director General
Economic Research and Regional Cooperation Department
Asian Development Bank

Acknowledgments

We would like to acknowledge the Asian Development Bank team for their generous help and support throughout this project: Shu Tian, Donghyun Park, Satoru Yamadera, Kosintr Puongsophol, and Mai Lin Villaruel. We would also like to thank Madeline Dixon for her excellent research assistance. Participants in the workshop on Developing Social Bond Markets in Asia: A Primer on Social Bonds, which was held on 8 October 2020, provided additional feedback and information that was very helpful, and we would like to acknowledge their support as well: Ulrich Volz, Mushtaq Kapasi, Ephyro Luis B. Amatong, Yoko Chivers, and Poonsit Wongthawatchai.

Abbreviations

ADB   Asian Development Bank
ASEAN   Association of Southeast Asian Nations
DIB   development impact bond
ESG   environmental, social, and governance
EUR   euro
GDP   gross domestic product
ICMA   International Capital Market Association
IMF   International Monetary Fund
JPY   Japanese yen
PRC   People's Republic of China
SBP   Social Bond Principles
SDG   Sustainable Development Goal
SIB   social impact bond
SMEs   small and medium-sized enterprises
SLB   sustainability-linked bond
UN   United Nations
USD   United States dollar

Economy Codes
AUS   Australia
FIJ   Fiji
GEO   Georgia
HKG   Hong Kong, China
IND   India
INO   Indonesia
JPN   Japan
KOR   Republic of Korea
MAL   Malaysia
NZL   New Zealand
PHI   Philippines
PRC   People's Republic China
SIN   Singapore
TAP   Taipei,China
THA   Thailand

Executive Summary

There are moments in time when financial, social, and economic challenges spur financial markets to new heights of innovation. This is such a moment, when the notion of blended finance—investing for both social and financial gain—has taken hold around the world. Harnessing the power of private capital to address compelling societal needs is critical to meeting these challenges in developing Asia.* Social bonds, which raise funds to create social as well as financial value, are instruments with a vital role to play in spurring recovery from the coronavirus disease (COVID-19) crisis as well as in supporting future socioeconomic progress.

By early 2020, around 25% of money under professional management was invested in assets that were aligned with social and/or environmental goals in addition to seeking financial returns. In response to growing investor demand for instruments that deliver environmental, social, and governance (ESG) value, equity and bond markets have innovated over the past 2 decades to develop a number of sustainable finance instruments. The global bond markets have embraced this movement; ESG bond issuance jumped to $330 billion in 2019, up 33% from 2018, and outstanding ESG bonds passed the $1 trillion threshold in the middle of 2020. While the ESG market initially was dominated by green bonds, which finance environmental projects, social bonds have experienced exceptional growth in 2020, partly due to the emergence of a new subset, COVID-19 bonds, which finance activities that mitigate the fallout from the pandemic. This development is ushering in a new era of explosive growth for ESG-linked bonds in general and social bonds in particular.

These promising developments in the arena of sustainable finance, however, have been accompanied by some confusion about terminology and guidelines in the ESG bond market. This paper uses the principles set out by the International Capital Market Association (ICMA) for specific types of ESG-focused, fixed-income instruments and will use the phrase "ESG bonds" to describe the entire universe of bonds that specify use of proceeds to seek ESG goals alongside financial value. The ICMA principles form the foundation for various standards throughout the world that have been adapted to address local trends and—in the case of the Association of Southeast Asian Nations Social Bond Standards—introduce special, additional features applicable to the region.

Under the ICMA framework, there are three types of ESG bond instruments: (i) green bonds, which raise capital for projects with environmental benefits; (ii) social bonds, which raise funds for projects with social benefits; and (iii) sustainability bonds, which raise funds for projects with both green and social benefits. More recently, the ICMA issued guidance on sustainability-linked bonds, which differ from the above in that their structure and financial outcomes are linked to the achievement of pre-agreed key performance indicators. In June 2020, the ICMA expanded its list of eligible projects and target communities relevant to social bonds in response to the rapid growth of the social bond market due to the COVID-19 pandemic.

---

* Developing Asia comprises the 46 developing member economies of the Asian Development Bank.

Economic and social development needs in developing Asia highlight the urgency of creating a robust social bond market in the region. With the stunning impact of COVID-19 still unfolding, the Asian Development Bank (ADB) expects the pandemic to take a heavy toll on the region's developing economies. In December 2020, ADB forecasts that developing Asia's gross domestic product would contract by 0.4% in 2020, the region's weakest economic performance since 1961. This is expected to be followed by a 6.8% expansion in 2021, which implies only a partial recovery, and with downside risks, rather than upside potential, prevailing. The fallout from the pandemic has been disproportionately damaging to vulnerable and underserved people and communities throughout the region, as vital areas such as tourism, the informal economy, and small and medium-sized enterprises have staggered. This has exacerbated the funding gap needed to attain the United Nations Sustainable Development Goals. Prior to the pandemic, the United Nations warned that developing economies in Asia and the Pacific faced an annual funding gap of $1.5 trillion compared with what was needed to achieve the Sustainable Development Goals. These developments underscore the opportunity for social bonds to help close the funding gap by financing social investments and improving the quality of project outcomes through a commitment to measuring and reporting impact.

Global social bond issuance saw tremendous growth in 2020, as the COVID-19 pandemic and economic shutdowns greatly increased market supply and demand for financing response and recovery efforts. Following year-on-year growth of 28% in 2018 and 44% in 2019, the issuance of global social bonds surged to $149.4 billion equivalent in 2020, an eightfold increase from 2019.

Social bond issuance in Asia has consistently lagged behind European issuance, but recent growth in the region has been impressive. In 2017, Asian social bond issuance comprised 12% of total global (excluding supranational) issuance; its share grew to 23% of the global total in 2020. From 2017 to 2020, the Asian social bond market grew 22.3 times, compared with growth of 9.8 times for Europe and 14.3 times for the world excluding Asia. Nonetheless, the Asian social bond market is still barely more than a third of the size of the European market in terms of its global issuance share, and the need for even faster growth is urgent.

In the Asian social bond market, issuance so far has been dominated by government-related agency issuers in high-income economies such as Japan and the Republic of Korea, where such issuance makes up 41% and 49% of the entire outstanding Asian social bond market, respectively. Overall, the region has been relatively slow to adopt ICMA-compliant issuance, which is mainly limited to Australia, India, Japan, the Republic of Korea, the Philippines, Singapore, and Thailand. Growth of the social bond market in Asia is closely linked to investor interest in COVID-19-linked bonds.

This government-agency-led pattern of issuance reflects the relatively recent emergence of the global social bond market, as governments and supranational policy-driven issuers tend to be the first-to-market. They are followed by private financial and industrial issuers, and eventually sovereign and treasury issuers, in response to the broadening awareness and relevance of these instruments. In this sense, the global and Asian social bond markets are following the development path of the larger and more developed green bond market. Financial institution issuers make up the single-largest private sector source of supply in the social bond market, although this figure is still small at 16.2% for the global market and 10.5% for Asia (excluding supranational issuers). Nonfinancial corporate issuers make up only a small fraction of the global social bond market (excluding supranational issuers) at 3.0% globally and 2.9% in Asia.

To a large extent, investor demand has been the driving force behind growth in the social bond market. Globally, funds that buy ESG bonds grew by about 12% during the first half of 2020, reaching a record-high of $209.5 billion in assets according to data from Morningstar. Investors in ESG bonds may have several reasons to include ESG in their investment management process, including the value rationale, and a commitment to increasing transparency and governance.

While philanthropic and supranational institutions are significant issuers of social bonds, they also help to develop the market ecosystem and support prospective participants in entering the market. Governments, including both policymakers and regulators, also are key to ecosystem development. Together, these groups can provide market education, technical assistance, thought leadership, and an enabling regulatory framework; they can also take an active role in crowding in private capital by offering first-loss capital or guarantees of capital.

Looking at some characteristics of the social bond market, we see that currency composition is dominated by the euro (68.9%), although the Asian social bond market also includes regional currencies such as the Japanese yen and Korean won, which represent 7.6% and 4.3% of the global share, respectively. We estimate that the weighted average credit rating of the global social bond market is AA, compared with a weighted average of A+ in the global green bond market and AA– in the global sustainability bond market. We further estimate that the average issue size of current outstanding social bonds globally is now $540 million, including 2020's jumbo-sized deals, compared with $300 million for green bonds and $455 million for sustainability bonds.

In the Asian market, issuance is dominated by Japanese and Korean government-related issuers, as well as private sector financial issuers. Many Asian social bond issuers in 2020, however, were entirely new entrants to the ESG bond market. Meanwhile, social bond issuance in the People's Republic of China that is in line with internationally recognized standards such as ICMA guidelines is extremely limited.

It seems likely that both investors' and issuers' attraction to social bonds will not fade with COVID-19. Obstacles to market growth, however, include the lack of a standardized set of metrics to measure impact, which leads to concerns about "social washing" (i.e., overstating the social value of a bond); a need for higher issuance volume and diversity (i.e., more corporate issuers); a lack of training among financial advisers; and the lack of a social bond framework—which can take time, money, and human resources to develop—for many of Asia's sovereigns and corporates that would like to tap the market.

Philanthropic and multilateral institutions, as well as governments, can help to overcome these obstacles by lending their support to the market. Another opportunity is for the Islamic finance market to step up its contribution to ESG-linked funding. Gender lens investing can also help grow the social bond market by channeling investments toward the social and economic empowerment of women.

There is undoubtedly an urgent and compelling case for the development of a robust social bond market in Asia. Harnessing the power of private capital to meet critical social needs is an opportunity for both issuers and investors to address these needs in a financial context. While the COVID-19 pandemic will eventually fade away, one lasting impact may well be its catalytic effect on the development of social bonds worldwide. There is an opportunity to use these innovative financial instruments to direct private capital to address long-standing social ills even as the pandemic eases and a new global normal emerges.

Introduction—An Opportunity for Financial Innovation

1

There are moments in time when the world is ripe with opportunity. In the world of finance, great innovations often arise from such moments. Financial guidelines and structures were born in the wake of the Great Depression, paving the way for massive growth and prosperity over the next century. In the middle of the 20th century, government intervention in the home mortgage market empowered countless families to become homeowners. By the end of the 20th century, syndicated loans and project financing had enabled huge development projects, ranging from gold mines to the Suez Canal. These innovations arose from financial, social, and economic challenges that spurred financial markets to new heights of creativity.

Sometime around the dawn of the 21st century, another such moment arrived as long-held views on the role of finance in society began to evolve, and the notion of blended value took hold. As the gatekeepers to finance, lenders and investors are responsible for allocating scarce capital to the most promising sectors. Traditional business thinking held that these promising sectors were those most likely to maximize shareholder value. The interests of other stakeholders, including government and society, were considered for their nuisance value more than for their intrinsic worth.

In the past 2 decades, however, the notion of blended value investing—investing for both financial and social gain—has gained credence even among the most traditional of financial managers. As the CEO of investment giant BlackRock wrote in 2018: "To prosper over time, every company must not only deliver financial performance, but also show how it makes a positive contribution to society. Companies must benefit all of their stakeholders, including shareholders, employees, customers, and the communities in which they operate."[1] Blended value—which encompasses the social, environmental, governance, gender equity, and financial performance of a business—will only become more important in a globalized economy struggling to rebound from the effects of an unprecedented modern pandemic.

Now more than ever, harnessing the power of private capital to address compelling societal needs is critical to meeting economic and social challenges worldwide. This opportunity is especially promising for Asia. As Masatsugu Asakawa, President of the Asian Development Bank (ADB) points out, the region has already been a leader in fostering innovation of all sorts: "In the midst of such unprecedented economic disruption, innovative thinking is vital to overcome the current difficulties and rebound quickly."[2] To provide context for innovative solutions to this disruption, this paper will provide a primer on social bonds, an innovative financial instrument that offers both social and financial rewards. We will present the case for robust participation in the social bond market in Asia, where pressing needs align with growing investor demand.

---

[1] David Grayson. 2020. "Larry Fink, the FT, and Prince Charles are Right: It's Time for a Reset on Capitalism." Reuters. 27 January. https://www.reutersevents.com/sustainability/larry-fink-ft-and-prince-charles-are-right-its-time-reset-capitalism.

[2] Asian Development Bank (ADB). 2020. *Asian Development Outlook 2020: What Drives Innovation in Asia?* https://www.adb.org/sites/default/files/publication/575626/ado2020.pdf.

Outline of the Paper

The paper will begin by considering the historical and market context that forms the basis for the social bond market, especially investor interest in socially linked investments and the evolution of the market for sustainable finance. We will then discuss the taxonomy of bonds with environmental, social, and governance (ESG) goals, including a review of international and Asian regional guidelines for social bonds, as well as pay-for-success financial instruments. Next will come our perspective on why Asia needs a robust social bond market, with a look at economic and social development needs, the funding gap, and why social bonds are an instrument whose time has come.

The paper will then take a deeper dive into the specifics of the social bond market. We will explore market sizing and growth (both globally and in the Asian region), consider the differences between green bonds and social bonds, and delve into the development of coronavirus disease (COVID-19) social bonds in 2020. This will be followed by an in-depth examination of the various social bond market participants: issuers, investors, philanthropic organizations, supranationals, and governments.

Next will come a discussion of global and Asian social bond market characteristics. We will then consider the obstacles to social bond market growth in Asia and how these obstacles can be overcome. We will close with our vision of the way forward toward building a robust social bond market in Asia to advance socioeconomic development and recovery from the COVID-19 pandemic.

Historical and Market Context 2

In early 2020, research indicated that around 25% of money under professional management was invested in assets that were aligned with social and/or environmental goals in addition to financial returns. Moreover, institutional investors are increasingly seeking assets that incorporate socially responsible and environmental goals alongside financial returns. This can result in greater resilience to economic and market shocks, which offers downside risk protection that is valued by investors and can justify a pricing premium.[3]

In response to growing investor demand for socially responsible instruments, equity and bond markets have innovated to develop a number of sustainable finance instruments over the past 2 decades. In the equity world, impact investments seek to launch and build businesses that have a positive and measurable impact on society and the environment, while also earning a profit. Investments in solar energy, clean cookstoves, women-owned businesses, and affordable housing, for example, can fall into this category.

The bond markets too have increasingly embraced investor demand for ESG instruments within the broader umbrella of sustainable finance. In 2018, BloombergNEF found that a record $247 billion worth of sustainable finance bonds, based on a broad definition that includes environmental and social issues, came to market. In fact, since records began with the introduction of green bonds (i.e., environmentally focused) in 2007, the sustainable finance market has grown every year. ESG bond issuance jumped to around $330 billion in 2019, and outstanding ESG bonds passed the $1 trillion threshold in the middle of 2020.

The first "green" bond was issued by the European Investment Bank in 2007 as a "Climate Awareness Bond" for stimulating investment by institutional investors. The World Bank soon followed with the world's first labeled green bond in 2008, setting the stage for today's expanding and diversifying market in ESG bonds. These early green bonds were the result of interest from pension funds in Europe that were looking for ways to address global warming risks amid rising awareness following the Intergovernmental Panel on Climate Change Fourth Assessment Report in 2007. Soon other issuers, mainly multilateral lending organizations including ADB and the International Bank for Reconstruction and Development, joined this market with inaugural green bonds of their own. Without an accepted market standard, these early bonds were custom-designed on an organization-by-organization basis.

Market issuance of green bonds expanded rapidly from 2013, when the investable market tripled by outstanding face value each year. To meet the growing demand from investors for such instruments, the first green bond indices were launched in 2014, although overall green bond annual issuance did not exceed the $50 billion mark until 2016. Dedicated green bond funds are now widely available to investors in regions around the world, and annual issuance of green bonds grew to more than 3% of all global debt issuance in 2019, making these instruments a growing component of mainstream portfolios as well. Conversely, there are currently no social bond market indices available from mainstream index providers, and dedicated social bond funds are exceptionally rare.

---

[3] MSCI. 2018. Introducing ESG Investing. https://www.msci.com/documents/1296102/7943776/ESG+Investing+brochure.pdf/bcac11cb-872b-fe75-34b3-2eaca4526237.

International Capital Market Association (ICMA)-compliant social bond issuance experienced remarkable growth in 2020, increasing over eightfold from 2019's full-year total to $149.4 billion in 2020 (Figure 1). If the current level of growth and market diversification seen in 2020 continues in future years, then it is possible that the social bond market will follow the green bond market's development pattern in a reinforcing and sustainable cycle of issuance and investment.

In 2020, a new subset of social bonds, referred to as COVID-19 bonds, emerged to finance activities that mitigate the economic fallout from the pandemic. This development has ushered in a new era of explosive growth for ESG bonds in general and, as we will see below, social bonds in particular.

Figure 1: Global Social Bond Issuance by Year and Issuer Classification

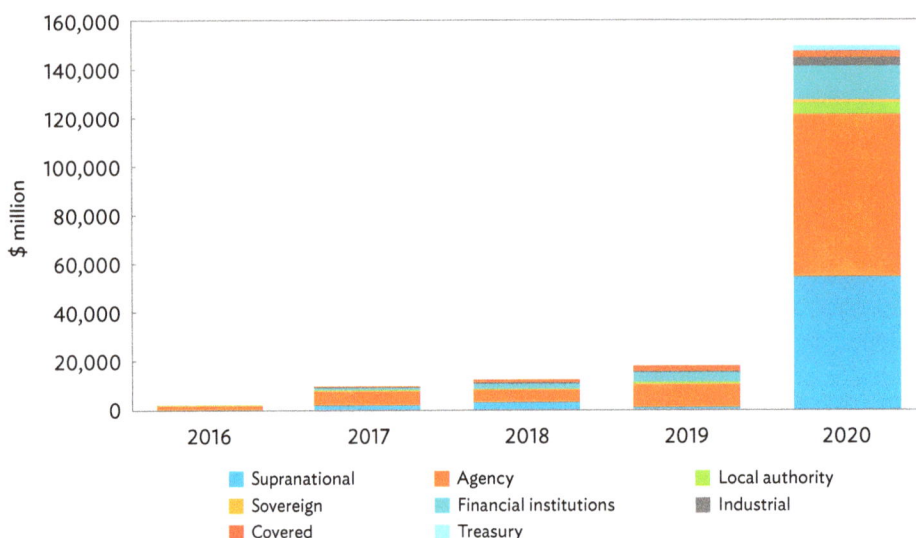

Note: Data for full-year 2020.
Source: Bloomberg LP.

Sustainable Finance—Taxonomy, Guidelines, and Principles

3

These promising developments in the arena of sustainable finance have been accompanied by widespread confusion about terminology and guidelines among participants, ranging from market experts to retail investors. For example, some use the terms "green bonds," "sustainable," "social impact," and "social" interchangeably despite significant differences between them. It is challenging to talk about precise definitions of the various ESG bond instruments because there is no single market consensus; and where there is consensus, it tends to vary by region. This paper will use the principles set out by the ICMA for specific types of sustainability-focused, fixed-income instruments and will use the term "ESG bonds" to describe the entire universe of bonds that specify use of proceeds to seek ESG goals alongside financial value.[4] The ICMA principles form the foundation for various standards throughout the world that have been adapted to address local trends and—in the case of the Association of Southeast Asian Nations (ASEAN) Capital Markets Forum—introduce special additional features applicable to the region.

ICMA Guidelines: Green, Social, and Sustainability Bonds

Perhaps viewing with alarm the potentially hazardous proliferation of ill-defined and ill-governed ESG bond instruments, in 2014 the ICMA issued the first version of the Green Bond Principles, followed by the Social Bond Principles (SBP) and Sustainability Bond Principles in 2017 (with the SBP most recently updated in June 2020). The ICMA approach is market-based rather than one of exhaustive definitions and taxonomies, reflecting the lack of consensus noted above. The ICMA created three categories of ESG bonds:

- **Green bonds** "enable capital-raising and investment for new and existing projects with environmental benefits";
- **Social bonds** are "use-of-proceeds bonds that raise funds for new and existing projects with positive social outcomes," such as improving food security and access to education, health care, and financial services; and
- **Sustainability bonds** are bonds for which "the proceeds will be exclusively applied to finance or re-finance a combination of both Green and Social projects."[5]

The ICMA also issued guidelines for each type of ESG bond, including the SBP:

The SBP are voluntary process guidelines that recommend transparency and disclosure and promote integrity in the development of the social bond market by clarifying the approach for issuance of a social bond. The SBP are intended for broad use by the market: they provide issuers

---

[4] This is different from the new ESG-linked or sustainability-linked bond format, which links the coupon to performance in agreed ESG factors.

[5] ICMA. 2018. *Sustainable Bond Guidelines*. https://www.icmagroup.org/assets/documents/Regulatory/Green-Bonds/Sustainability-Bonds-Guidelines-June-2018-270520.pdf.

with guidance on the key components involved in launching a credible social bond; they aid investors by promoting availability of information necessary to evaluate the positive impact of their social bond investments; and they assist underwriters by moving the market toward expected disclosures that will facilitate transactions.[6]

In response to the fast-growing COVID-19 bond market, on 10 June 2020, the ICMA expanded its list of eligible projects and target communities included in the SBP (Box 1).

Box 1: June 2020 Update to the International Capital Market Association Social Bond Principles

Social project categories include, but are not limited to, providing and/or promoting the following:

- affordable basic infrastructure (e.g., clean drinking water, sewers, sanitation, transport, and energy);
- access to essential services (e.g., education and vocational training, health care, financing, and financial services);
- affordable housing;
- employment generation and programs designed to prevent and/or alleviate unemployment stemming from socioeconomic crises, including through the potential effect of financing micro, small, and medium-sized enterprises;
- food security and sustainable food systems (e.g., physical, social, and economic access to safe, nutritious, and sufficient food that meets dietary needs and requirements); resilient agricultural practices; reduction of food loss and waste; and improved productivity of small-scale producers; and
- socioeconomic advancement and empowerment (e.g., equitable access to and control over assets, services, resources, and opportunities; and equitable participation and integration into the market and society, including the reduction of income inequality).

Target populations include, but are not limited to, the following:

- those living below the poverty line,
- excluded and/or marginalized populations and/or communities,
- people with disabilities,
- migrants and/or displaced persons,
- the undereducated,
- the underserved (owing to a lack of quality access to essential goods and services),
- the unemployed,
- women and/or sexual and gender minorities, and
- aging populations and vulnerable youth.

Source: International Capital Market Association Social Bond Principles.

---

[6] ICMA. 2018. *Social Bond Principles*. https://www.icmagroup.org/assets/documents/Regulatory/Green-Bonds/June-2020/Social-Bond-PrinciplesJune-2020-090620.pdf.

ASEAN Social Bond Standards

In 2018, the ASEAN Capital Markets Forum developed the ASEAN Social Bond Standards to complement the ASEAN Green Bond Standards introduced the previous year. The ASEAN Social Bond Standards are based on the ICMA SBP described earlier; however, they provide more specific guidelines on the use of proceeds to reflect the ASEAN region's social and religious diversity.

Specifically, key additional features of the ASEAN Social Bond Standards include the following:

- **Eligible issuers.** The issuer of a social bond must have a geographic or economic connection to the ASEAN region.
- **Ineligible projects.** Projects that involve alcohol, gambling, tobacco, and weapons are excluded from the ASEAN Social Bond Standards.
- **Continuous accessibility to information.** Investors should be able to access information continuously. Therefore, issuers are required to disclose information, in both the issuance documentation and a public website, on the use of proceeds, process for project evaluation and selection, and management of proceeds.
- **Encouragement of more frequent reporting.** In addition to the annual reports, issuers are encouraged to provide more frequent reporting to improve transparency on the use of proceeds and investor confidence.
- **External review.** Engaging an external reviewer is voluntary, as under the ICMA guidelines. However, the ASEAN Social Bond Standards require external reviewers to have "relevant expertise and experience in the area which they are reviewing," which is to be disclosed on a publicly accessible website.[7]

Pay-for-Success Instruments

In line with the growth of ESG bonds thus far in the 21st century, another set of financial instruments has emerged that is based on the principle of pay-for-success: social impact bonds (SIBs), development impact bonds (DIBs), and sustainability-linked bonds (SLBs). Not to be confused with the earlier discussion on ESG-linked bonds, SIBs and DIBs are a very small and different set of instruments, which are not really bonds at all. Rather, they are public–private partnerships based on an agreement that investors will receive a return of their principal plus some financial return if and only if the project achieves a predetermined rate of success on social and/or environmental goals. These are best understood as pay-for-success projects, where success is defined as the achievement of socially beneficial goals such as improved early childhood health or higher employment rates among at-risk youth. In a SIB, government is the outcomes funder who repays investors when success is achieved; in a DIB, the outcomes funder is a nongovernmental entity such as a philanthropic organization or multilateral development bank.

In addition, SLBs are instruments based on key performance indicators, sometimes including the United Nations (UN) Sustainable Development Goals (SDGs) (Table 1). SLBs are issued with a structural component, such as the coupon, that varies depending on whether or not a defined ESG objective is achieved. The ICMA issued a set of principles for SLBs in 2020. SLBs also differ from the ESG bonds described earlier in that funds raised through SLBs are used for general corporate purposes rather than for specific project(s).

---

[7] ASEAN Capital Markets Forum. 2018. *ASEAN Social Bond Standards.* https://www.sc.com.my/api/documentms/download. ashx?id=27ab0a48-b429-4874-93ae-35248ebea3e6#:~:text=To%20support%20ASEAN's%20sustainable%20development,first%20 introduced%20in%20November%202017.

Table 1: Quick Guide to Different Types of Instruments

	SIB	DIB	Sustainability Bond	Social Bond	SLB
Is bond performance linked to success on ESG objectives (pay-for-success)?	Yes; investor is paid back principal plus interest if and only if pre-agreed outcomes are achieved.	Yes; investor is paid back principal plus interest if and only if pre-agreed outcomes are achieved.	No	No	Yes; KPIs are selected; structural and/or financial characteristics vary depending on whether the KPIs are achieved.
Investors	Some mainstream; mostly philanthropic	Virtually all philanthropic	Mainstream investors with ESG lens	Mainstream investors with social lens	Unclear (none issued in Asia yet)
Use-of-Proceeds	Specific ESG-based project	Specific ESG-based project	Projects with green and social goals	Projects with social goals	General corporate purposes
Guidelines	No	No	ICMA Sustainability Bond Principles (2018)	ICMA Social Bond Principles (2017; updated June 2020)	ICMA Sustainability-Linked Bond Principles (June 2020)
Outcomes Payor	Usually government	Not government; usually a philanthropy or supranational	N.A.	N.A.	N.A.

DIB = development impact bond; ESG = environmental, social, and governance; ICMA = International Capital Market Association; KPI = key performance indicator; N.A. = not applicable; SIB = social impact bond, SLB = sustainability-linked bond.
Source: Authors' compilation.

The first such bond was issued in 2019, but additional activity has been minimal and thus far no Asian issuer has launched an SLB.

The first SIB was launched in the United Kingdom in 2010; after 10 years of much-hyped growth, total issuance through the middle of 2020 was still insignificant at about $400 million (Table 2). SIBs and DIBs suffer from many deficiencies, including (i) a dependence on philanthropy to fund outsize project development costs, (ii) complexity, (iii) small size, (iv) the potential for adverse consequences, and (v) a spotty track record. As a result, this paper will not consider SIBs as a viable sustainable finance instrument at scale for developing Asia.[8]

---

[8] Information on SIBs and DIBs is available on the websites of Social Finance at www.socialfinance.org.uk and the Brookings Institution at https://www.brookings.edu/series/impact-bonds/.

Table 2: Social Impact Bonds versus Environmental, Social, and Governance Bonds

SIBs	ESG Bonds
Not true bonds	Bonds
Based on PFS	Not usually PFS
Variable return	Fixed income
May have guarantee of principal	Usually no guarantees
Impact-first investors	Mainstream investors
Long development time	Quick issuance
$400 million in issuance in 10 years	$384 billion in issuance in 2020[a]

ESG = environmental, social, and governance; PFS = pay-for-success; SIB = social impact bond.

[a] Issuance in 2020 for January through the middle of November.

Source: Authors' compilation.

Urgent Need for a Robust Social Bond Market in Asia

4

Economic Development Needs

Even before the COVID-19 pandemic, the UN estimated that meeting the 17 SDGs would require global investments of $5 trillion–$7 trillion per annum through 2030, implying that there is a huge funding gap that only the public and private sectors working together can fill.

The pandemic has upended those estimates. Based on its October 2020 estimate, the International Monetary Fund (IMF) expects a 4.4% contraction in global gross domestic product (GDP) in 2020 even after the announcement of economic stimulus measures from governments. The IMF anticipates that the pandemic will leave medium-term scars as well, warning that "the cumulative loss in global output relative to the pre-pandemic projected path is projected to grow from $11 trillion over 2020–2021 to $28 trillion over 2020–2025," which represents a "severe setback to the improvement in average living standards across all country groups."[9]

The need to shore up their sagging economies will take an especially heavy toll on the budgets of developing countries. According to the IMF, these countries will have added 5.5 percentage points of GDP to their fiscal deficits and 6.8 percentage points to their public debt levels in 2020.[10]

With the stunning impact of COVID-19 still unfolding, ADB expects the pandemic to take a heavy toll on Asia's developing economies. While some economies were exiting lockdowns by the middle of 2020, the lingering disruptions to global supply chains, tourism, and workers' remittances are among the many factors that will dampen growth for the year. In nine Asian economies with available data, tourism arrival declines in April 2020 ranged from 87% to 100% compared with the previous year. Those economies that are heavily tourism-reliant are probably not going to see visitors return to pre-pandemic levels for several years.

ADB estimated in December 2020 that developing Asia's GDP would contract by 0.4% in 2020, the region's weakest performance since 1961; this is expected to be followed by a 6.8% expansion in 2021 (Table 3). Excluding newly industrialized economies, regional GDP is projected to fall by 0.3% in 2020 before returning to growth of 7.2% in 2021. Economic performance has been uneven across the region, with Thailand, India, and the Philippines among the hardest-hit economies, and Viet Nam much less affected. One major engine of growth in developing Asia, the People's Republic of China (PRC), saw an estimated GDP expansion of just 2.1% in 2020 but is expected to rebound to grow 7.7% in 2021. Another regional growth engine, India, contracted by an estimated 8.0% in fiscal year 2020 and is expected to post a recovery to 8.0% growth from this

---

[9] G. Gopinath. 2020. "A Long, Uneven and Uncertain Ascent." *IMF Blog.* 13 October. https://blogs.imf.org/2020/10/13/a-long-uneven-and-uncertain-ascent/.

[10] G. Gopinath and V. Gaspar. 2020. "Fiscal Policies for a Transformed World." *IMF Blog.* 10 July. https://blogs.imf.org/2020/07/10/fiscal-policies-for-a-transformed-world/.

Table 3: Gross Domestic Product Growth Forecasts in Asia

Region	2020	2021
Central Asia	−2.1	3.8
East Asia	1.6	7.0
South Asia	−6.1	7.2
Southeast Asia	−4.4	5.2
The Pacific	−6.1	1.3
Developing Asia	**−0.4**	**6.8**
Selected Economies		
Malaysia	−6.0	7.0
Philippines	−8.5	6.5
Thailand	−7.8	4.0
Viet Nam	2.3	6.1
India	−8.0	8.0
Hong Kong, China	−5.5	5.1
People's Republic of China	2.1	7.7

Source: Asian Development Bank. 2020. *Asian Development Outlook Supplement December.* https://www.adb.org/sites/default/files/publication/658721/ado-supplement-december-2020.pdf.

lower base in fiscal year 2021.[11] As ADB warned in its *Asian Development Outlook 2020 Update* in September: "This will not be a V-shaped recovery. Continued social distancing will hamper activity, and recurrent outbreaks are possible. Even if an individual economy succeeds in normalizing domestic activity, it will face an environment of very weak external demand… Risks to the outlook remain on the downside."[12]

According to the Organisation for Economic Co-operation and Development, governments in emerging Asia "have adopted fiscal stimulus policies of unprecedented proportions, and policy makers have ramped up monetary accommodation." While this Keynesian stimulus is not only reasonable but necessary, it does pose the risk of unmanageable budget deficits and debt service requirements further down the line. The Organisation for Economic Co-operation and Development report adds: "With emerging Asia highly susceptible to natural hazards such as storms and flooding, particularly in the second half of the year, many governments in the region will be hard-pressed to manage the increase in their initially planned fiscal deficit ratios."[13]

Social Development Needs

The COVID-19 pandemic threatens to erase many of the hard-won gains in social development indicators in Asia. Gig workers and those in the informal economy, for example, have been hard-hit by the lockdown as street vendors and small and medium-sized enterprises (SMEs) struggle to survive. As noted above, the

---

[11] ADB. 2020. *Asian Development Outlook Supplement December.* https://www.adb.org/sites/default/files/publication/658721/ado-supplement-december-2020.pdf.

[12] ADB. 2020. *Asian Development Outlook Update: Wellness in Worrying Times.* https://www.adb.org/sites/default/files/publication/635666/ado2020-update.pdf.

[13] Organisation for Economic Co-operation and Development. 2020. *Economic Outlook for Southeast Asia, China, and India 2020—Update: Meeting the Challenges of COVID-19.* https://www.oecd-ilibrary.org/development/economic-outlook-for-southeast-asia-china-and-india_23101113.

tourism industry has staggered under the blow of the pandemic, while global manufacturing also slowed due to declining demand and supply chain disruptions. This is why financing for SMEs affected by COVID-19 has been such a large part of social bond issuance to date.

As fiscal revenues collapse and crisis-response spending and debt grow, public resources that can be allocated to long-term issues like climate change and education are shrinking. Thus, there is an enormous funding gap that social bonds can fill.

The COVID-19 pandemic has also exposed the depth and importance of the digital divide. Broadband access for disadvantaged populations (or the lack thereof) has always been one of the use-of-proceed areas for social bonds, but the COVID-19 crisis has made this need much more immediate and pressing. Addressing this issue is likely to become even more imperative as some of the shift to more virtual education and work is likely to become permanent—a compelling illustration of how the original SBP have been given new meaning and urgency by the COVID-19 crisis.

Funding Gap

With just 10 years remaining to achieve the ambitious SDGs, developing economies face a severe funding gap that is being exacerbated by the pandemic. Even more worrisome, much of the private sector investment in developing economies focuses on middle- and high-income emerging markets, leaving lower-income economies even farther from reaching their goals.

The UN Conference on Trade and Development estimates that $5 trillion–$7 trillion per annum will be required to achieve the SDGs by 2030, including $3.3 trillion–$4.5 trillion in developing economies. This leaves an annual funding shortfall of around $2.5 trillion globally. The UN has warned that developing economies in Asia and the Pacific will need to invest an additional $1.5 trillion per annum, or 5% of their combined GDP, to achieve the SDGs.[14] Funds are desperately needed for power, transport, digital infrastructure, climate change mitigation, health care, education, food security, water and sanitation, and more. A 2014 Ceres report warned that the world needs to invest an additional $1 trillion per year for the next 36 years to avoid the worst effects of climate change alone.[15] With official development assistance at perhaps $150 billion per year and workers' remittances at around $450 billion, the need for private capital to fill this gap is both obvious and dramatic.

And then COVID-19 arrived, with devastating effects on public sector finances and a sharp deterioration in living conditions for the most vulnerable communities around the world. This pandemic's impact is a double-edged sword: it has both enlarged the funding gap and made more urgent the need for private capital to address these challenges.

---

[14] United Nations Economic and Social Commission for Asia and the Pacific. 2019. *United Nations' Regional Arm Explores A New Financial Landscape For Asia And The Pacific.* https://www.unescap.org/news/united-nations-regional-arm-explores-new-financial-landscape-asia-and-pacific#:~:text=%E2%80%9CESCAP%20has%20estimated%20that%20developing,achieve%20the%20SDGs%20by%20 2030.&text=The%20funding%20gap%20for%20countries,per%20cent%20of%20the%20GDP.

[15] Ceres. January 2014. *Investing in the Clean Trillion: Closing the Clean Energy Investment Gap.* https://www.ceres.org/resources/reports/ investing-clean-trillion-closing-clean-energy-investment-gap.

Why Social Bonds?

In terms of the broader financial landscape, social bonds are an attractive instrument for helping to close the funding gap by financing social investments. Since the issuer of a social bond commits to measuring and reporting its impact, the quality of project outcomes is likely to be enhanced due to this greater scrutiny. This aspect of social bonds is particularly valuable for the not-for-profit (e.g., government and agency) issuers whose missions tend to be most aligned to social financing needs—and who are the most active issuers of social bonds.

At the sovereign level, as opposed to the agency level where an organization's mission tends to be more focused (e.g., housing or SME financing), anecdotal experience from green bond issuers indicates that a significant level of organizational coordination is involved in linking typically unrelated departments such as finance and environmental ministries. This may pose a challenge at first, but it can lead to more effective use of data and resource management. Similar synergies may be possible in the social bond market as well, which investors may assess positively in terms of governance quality. Also, the publicity and awareness that accompanies social bond issuance may present a unique opportunity for nonprofit organizations or government agencies to communicate the importance of their social mission to investors, stakeholders, and policy makers alike.

Social bonds may also present a unique opportunity for better governance in bond markets, since issuance of these bonds goes hand in hand with disclosure of corporate or government activities and use of proceeds. As a result, issuers and investors can see a clearer linkage between funding and use of the money—a significant effect in the developing market context where a lack of transparency can be problematic. Thus, social bonds can create a direct impact such as improved healthcare or education, while also creating an indirect impact through increased transparency.

Market Sizing and Growth: Global Markets

Global social bond issuance saw tremendous growth in 2020, as the COVID-19 pandemic and economic shutdowns greatly increased the market supply and demand for financing response and recovery efforts. Following year-on-year growth of about 28% in 2018 and about 44% in 2019, the total issuance of global ICMA-compliant social bonds surged by 720% in 2020 to the equivalent of $149.4 billion in 2020, compared with $18.2 billion of issuance in 2019 (Table 4). The cost of issuing these bonds may be slightly higher than for straight bonds, due to framework development, review, and reporting requirements; however, investors are increasingly allocating capital and placing value on these attributes.

S&P Global believed that social bonds would be the fastest-growing segment of the ESG bond market in 2020, in contrast to lower issuance volume in the rest of the global fixed-income market. In 2019, social bonds made up only 5% of total sustainable debt issuance. This percentage grew sharply in 2020, with social bonds accounting for over 30% of total market issuance.[16]

Table 4: Monthly Global Social Bond Issuance in 2020

Month	Count	Total Amount Issued ($ million)
January	10	2,855
February	14	4,419
March	15	3,090
April	20	10,530
May	13	7,763
June	24	12,348
July	17	9,787
August	10	1,381
September	30	16,734
October	28	38,790
November	18	24,578
December	13	17,102
Total	**212**	**149,377**

Note: Data include only International Capital Market Association-compliant, publicly listed social bonds.
Source: Bloomberg LP.

[16] S&P Global. 2020. *A Pandemic-Driven Surge In Social Bond Issuance Shows The Sustainable Debt Market Is Evolving.* 22 June. https://www.spglobal.com/ratings/en/research/articles/200622-a-pandemic-driven-surge-in-social-bond-issuance-shows-the-sustainable-debt-market-is-evolving-11539807.

Global social bond issuance in the third quarter of 2020 reached $27.9 billion, up nearly threefold from $10.4 billion in the first quarter, with European issuers and financial institutions accounting for nearly two-thirds of issuance. Social bond issuance in the fourth quarter of 2020 reached a record $80.5 billion. Social bonds are now a key driver of market growth, as total ESG bond issuance reached $100.3 billion in the second quarter of 2020—a 65% jump from the previous year—mainly due to increased issuance of social bonds.[17]

As noted above, the COVID-19 pandemic has given rise to a dramatic increase in social bond issuance worldwide. It is not clear yet whether social bond issuance will slacken as the immediate shock of the pandemic eases, or whether the pipeline is still quite full; but nonetheless, 2020 was a record year for social bonds.

Market Sizing and Growth: Asian Markets

Annual social bond issuance data, broken down by World Bank region, reveal that Asia (East Asia, the Pacific, and South Asia) has consistently lagged behind Europe (Europe and Central Asia) in recent years, including in 2020. North America has seen few social bonds, reflecting its consistent tendency to lag behind Europe in its commitment to green and social financing. However, annual social bond issuance from Asia has grown to such a degree than it is now the second-largest region (excluding issuance by supranational entities) for social bond issuance in the world by a considerable margin (Figure 2).

Figure 2: Global Social Bond Issuance by Year and Region of Issuer

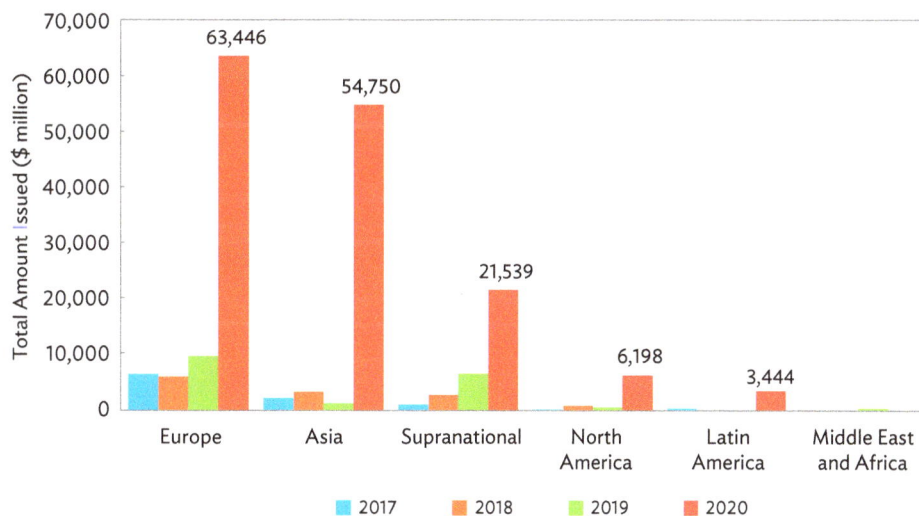

Notes: Data represent the annual sum of issuance in United States dollar equivalent. Data for full-year 2020.
Source: Bloomberg LP.

---

[17] S. Slater. 2020. "Social Bond Issuance Surges to Record in Q2." *Nasdaq*. 21 August. https://www.nasdaq.com/articles/social-bond-issuance-surges-to-record-in-q2-2020-08-21.

Indeed, the recent growth of this market in Asia has been impressive. In 2017, the year before the ICMA SBP were first released, Asian social bond issuance comprised only 12% of global (excluding supranational) annual issuance; this figure had grown to 23% in 2020 (Figure 3). These figures represent a 22.3 times increase in issuance in the Asian social bond market from 2017 to 2020, compared with growth of 9.8 times for Europe and 14.3 times globally ex-Asia (Figure 4).

Figure 3: Global Social Bond Issuance by Region of Issuer

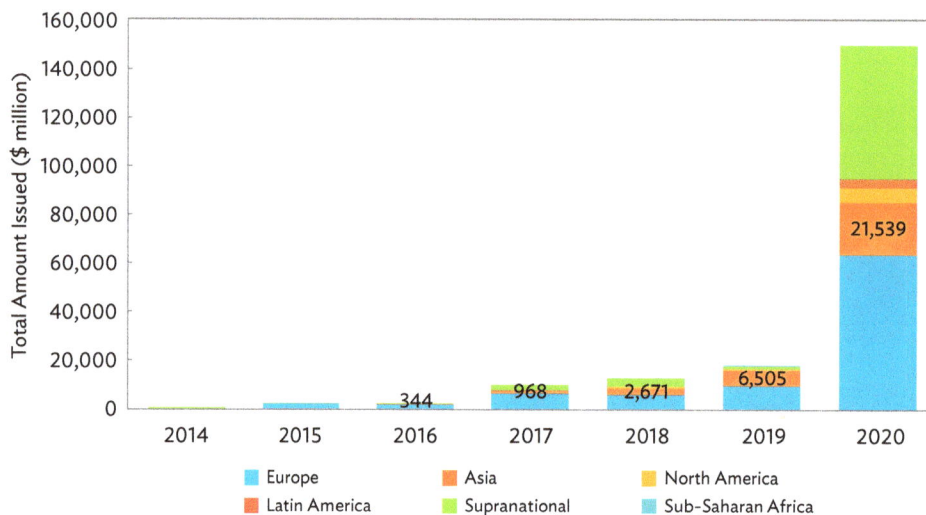

Notes: Data represent the annual sum of issuance in United States dollar equivalent. Data for full-year 2020.
Source: Bloomberg LP.

Figure 4: Growth in Annual Social Bond Issuance by Region, 2017 versus 2020

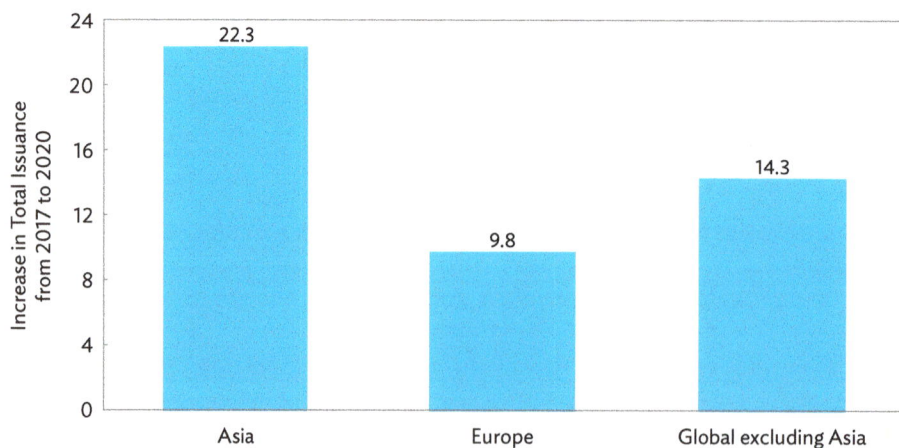

Note: Data for full-year 2020.
Source: Bloomberg LP.

In absolute terms, the amount of Asian ESG bond issuance remains a fraction of the global total for ESG bond issuance, comprising only 14.4% of the 2020 global total, including supranational issues. However, a somewhat different and more nuanced picture emerges when ESG bond issuance is broken down and compared on a relative share basis. From this perspective, Asia's social bond issuance in 2020 was 28.1% of the region's total ESG bond issuance, compared with 24.4% for non-Asian issuers, revealing rapid growth in both year-on-year and relative terms (Figure 5). Although this partly reflects the drop-off in green bond issuance in the PRC and does not count local currency COVID-19 bonds in the PRC, one possible interpretation of the data is that the social bond structure proved especially popular and well-suited to Asian markets in 2020.

Figure 5: Green, Social, and Sustainability Bonds as Shares of Annual ESG Bond Issuance for Asian and Non-Asian Issuers

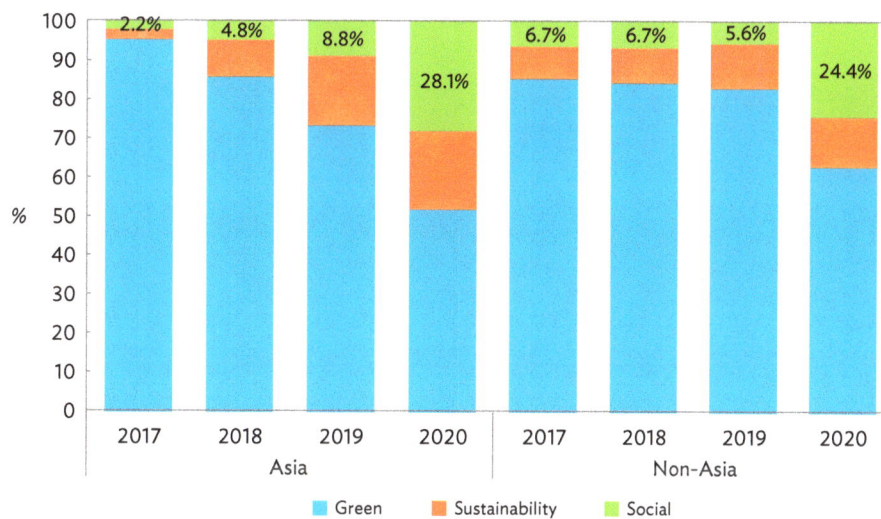

ESG = environmental, social, and governance.
Source: Bloomberg LP.

Nonetheless, the Asian social bond market is still barely one-third the size of the European market in terms of annual issuance, and the need for even faster growth in Asia is urgent. This is especially true for Asia's developing economies, as regional growth is almost entirely concentrated in its high-income economies. In fact, social bond issuance from 2017 to 2020 in Asia's high-income economies—led by the Republic of Korea and Japan—represented 94% of total Asian social bond issuance during this period (Figure 6). In 2019, no ICMA-compliant, publicly listed social bonds were issued in non-high-income Asian economies, reflecting a striking gap between the sources of and needs for social financing.

Figure 6: Social Bond Issuance in High-Income versus Non-High-Income Economies in Asia, 2017–2020

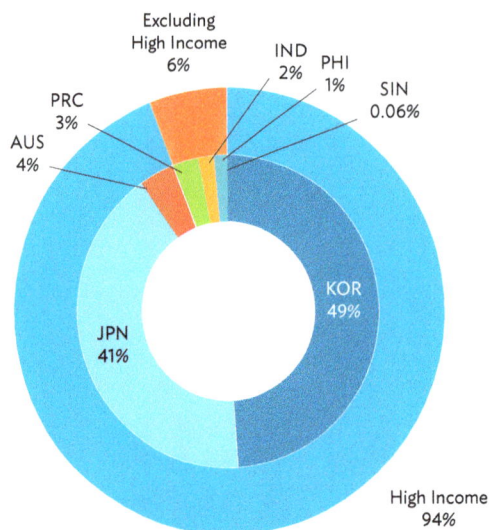

AUS = Australia, IND = India, JPN = Japan, KOR = Republic of Korea, PHI = Philippines, PRC = People's Republic of China, SIN = Singapore.
Notes: Based on World Bank income classifications. Issuance data for full-year 2020.
Source: Bloomberg LP.

Green Bonds versus Social Bonds

In the world of ESG bonds, the green bond market was the first to take off. However, in the era of COVID-19, social bonds are quickly proving to be the right innovation at the right moment in time.

Until 2020, green bonds comprised a large majority of total market issuance, while social bonds and sustainability bonds lagged far behind (Table 5). In 2019, green bond issuance was over $200 billion, compared with just $55 billion for social and sustainability bonds combined.

Green bonds probably owe their early lead in the issuance count to two factors: investor demand and the relative ease of impact measurement. Issuers have learned that "greening" their bond issue adds to its perceived value in the eyes of many investors without increasing risk, since the green bonds are pari passu (i.e., assets that are treated equally) to the issuer's nongreen bonds. Moreover, impact measurement for green bonds can be relatively straightforward and based on a quantifiable and generally standardized set of data such as the reduction in metric tons of carbon dioxide equivalent emissions, a modal shift in passenger miles, or the number of kilowatt-hours of renewable energy generated. This increases investor certainty that their funds are actually helping to achieve real environmental improvements in a verifiable way, rather than just "greenwashing" (i.e., making a project look more environmentally sound than it actually is).

Green bond assets and projects are also easier for issuers to identify and ring-fence than social bonds. This is because green bond projects easily lend themselves to, for example, technology, energy, infrastructure, or real estate portfolios. Accordingly, some institutional investors have established dedicated green bond portfolios,

Table 5: Green, Social, and Sustainability Bond Issuances

Year	Green Bonds	Social Bonds	Sustainability Bonds	Total Issuances
2007	1			1
2008	7		1	8
2009	13	1		14
2010	55	1		56
2011	30	1		31
2012	22	4	2	28
2013	40	2		42
2014	134	3	5	142
2015	303	3	6	312
2016	257	14	13	284
2017	434	42	18	494
2018	543	34	31	608
2019	779	66	86	931
2020	886	212	152	1,250
Total	**3,504**	**383**	**314**	**4,201**

Notes: Data include only International Capital Market Association-compliant, publicly listed bonds. Data for full-year 2020.

Source: Bloomberg LP.

responding to studies finding that a solid—and increasing—majority of investors want their portfolios to contribute to the battle against climate change.

Also, the green bond market is relatively much larger and more diversified than the social bond market, which has typically been exceptionally niche in terms of size and issuer diversity. On the other hand, green bond portfolios remain extremely small relative to total portfolios due both to supply and demand constraints. It may be that mainstream investors are increasingly willing and happy to hold green bonds as part of their overall portfolios, rather than pursue green-bond-specific portfolios. In fact, the majority of green bonds are held in nongreen bond funds and exchange-traded funds.

COVID-19 Social Bonds

The COVID-19 crisis has refocused public and private sector attention worldwide on social challenges such as unequal access to healthcare, the vulnerability of marginalized populations to systemic shocks, and the urgent need for private sector involvement to address these challenges. The pandemic has highlighted specific areas that can be addressed by social bonds, from medical research and production to SME financing for struggling businesses, and to revitalizing rural areas to accommodate an expected increase in remote working. Indeed, the COVID-19 impact is expanding and giving new meaning to the social bond format. There really has been a surprising amount of good innovation; the movement goes far beyond financing for vaccines and masks. Thus, activists, stockholders, and employees alike are pushing corporations into adding a social and environmental lens to their business strategy, products, and services. Investors are demanding concrete action and verifiable results, and they are increasingly checking that corporate actions and behavior during the crisis are aligned with their ESG and corporate social responsibility principles.

The COVID-19 pandemic poses a unique threat to progress on human development indicators such as poverty and inequality. But like all challenges, the pandemic also contains an embedded opportunity: to accelerate and mainstream the use of blended finance instruments like social bonds. It has provided a cohesive and powerful organizing theme for social bonds, much as climate change did for green bonds, where there was not a well-defined common theme pre-pandemic.

Accordingly, the pandemic has dramatically changed the landscape of the ESG bond market, increasing issuer and investor interest in social bonds relative to green bonds. The fearsome impact of the pandemic on health and economies worldwide has focused attention on innovative financial instruments that target both social and financial returns simultaneously—in other words, social bonds. Moreover, COVID-19 has suddenly generated a large supply of financing needs and a large pool of social assets and projects that can be financed by social bonds.

According to credit analysis from S&P Global:

> Increased unemployment, rising fatality rates, and strained health care systems have placed a spotlight on a future fraught with social risks. In parallel, corporations and financial institutions have been looked to for leadership in addressing these unforeseen challenges. This call for a greater focus on mitigating social risks has spilled over into the capital markets, particularly through the rapid rise of social bond issuance, which has more than quadrupled so far this year... [Growth in social bonds has far outpaced that of green bonds in 2020], portending a pivot away from a historically climate-centric sustainable debt space and reflecting a diversification of sustainability objectives financed by investors. And, while the recent surge may have been precipitated by COVID-19, the appeal of social bonds as a sustainable finance instrument may endure long after its effects have subsided.[18]

The main factor that has constrained ESG bond issuance is not the demand side, but the supply side. Corporate issuers like banks and nonfinancial issuers have to find assets on their balance sheets or eligible projects that meet the issuing principles, which is considerably easier for green projects (typically things) than for social projects (typically people). In this context, COVID-19 may be seen as the "global climate change for social bonds," because it is a big global issue that grabs attention and, crucially, is investable. The social bond concept has found new meaning as an optimal framework for raising funds to mitigate the devastating economic impact of COVID-19. Thus, this is very much the right time and right place for such financial innovation to thrive.

In April 2020, for example, the Government of Indonesia issued COVID-19 bonds at a time of historically high risk and a market selloff. It was the largest tranche of United States (US) dollar bonds ever issued by Indonesia, and it was its first ever 50-year issue of US dollar bonds. Nonetheless, the deal was successfully priced and sold to eager investors despite these risk factors, with the COVID-19-financing tag very likely making the bond more attractive for investors.

As we consider these pandemic-related opportunities, it is important to recognize that many of the so-called COVID-19 relief bonds are not technically social bonds because they do not adhere to the ICMA SBP, which, among other things, require transparency in the form of confirmed utilization of bonds' proceeds for projects with social benefits. Issuers need time to prepare social bond frameworks before they can go to market, so this may be a short-term phenomenon.

Some issuers are applying the Sustainability Bond Principles instead, in which proceeds can be used for a mix of social and environmental purposes, while others have invented their own labels and guidelines. Large

---

[18] Footnote 15.

institutional asset managers generally prefer bonds issued under the ICMA framework as they may offer greater accountability and support market quality standards.[19] This is especially the case in emerging markets like those in Asia, where governance and transparency risks are elevated, and where local standards are generally assumed to be less stringent than internationally recognized guidelines.

In June 2020, the ICMA updated its SBP to include an expanded list of social project categories and target populations. For COVID-19-themed social bonds, the updated ICMA recommendations note the following: "Illustrative examples for eligible social projects can include, for example, COVID-19-related expenditures to increase capacity and efficiency in provisioning healthcare services and equipment, medical research, SME loans that support employment generation in affected small businesses, and projects specifically designed to prevent and/or alleviate unemployment stemming from the pandemic."[20]

---

[19] Developing Asia comprises the 46 developing member economies of the Asian Development Bank. T. Freke and C. Mutua. 2019. "Who Put the "S" in "ESG" (and What Does It Mean)?" *Bloomberg*. 8 December. https://www.bloomberg.com/news/articles/2019-12-08/who-put-the-s-in-esg-and-what-does-it-mean-quicktake.

[20] ICMA. 2020. Q&A for Social Bonds Related to COVID-19. https://www.icmagroup.org/assets/documents/Regulatory/Green-Bonds/Social-Bonds-Covid-QA310320.pdf.

Social Bond Market Participants

6

As we explore the development of the ESG bond market in general, and social bonds specifically, it is important to understand the dynamics among the various market participants. Continued and sustainable growth of the social bond market will benefit from greater awareness and understanding of the potential of this market by issuers, investors, philanthropists, and policy makers and regulators.

Issuers

ADB was an early mover in Asia and the Pacific in adopting ESG bonds, which it called "theme bonds." Pierre Van Peteghem, ADB's treasurer, noted the following: "Our theme bonds highlight specific areas of the ADB's operations. Such themes have included water, gender, and health, of which we have issued over $2.7 billion since 2010."[21]

Increasingly, debt issuers are choosing to tap into the global trend for ESG investments by issuing bonds with an ESG label in response to growing investor demand. In 2020, investor interest and demand for COVID-19-linked bonds was particularly strong in Asia and the Pacific.

Government-Agency-Led Social Bond Issuers

The largest issuers in the global social bond market are government agencies including special purpose banks and lending agencies, which account for 46% of the total US-dollar-equivalent amount.[22] They are followed by supranational issuers—such as multilateral lending institutions, multilateral development banks, and others like the European Commission—at 32% and private sector financial institutions at 11% (Figure 7). Within Asia, the preponderance of government agency issuance is even more pronounced at 76% of the total outstanding bond stock (Figure 8).[23]

---

[21] J. Rogers. 2020. "Social Bonds on the Front Line." *HSBC*. 11 May. https://www.gbm.hsbc.com/insights/growth/social-bonds-on-the-front-line.

[22] The notional amount of a financial instrument is the nominal or face value that is used to calculate payments made on that instrument. This amount generally does not change and is thus referred to as notional.

[23] The various agency bond designations include the following:
- Agency–Government Guaranteed: A government agency backed by the full faith and credit of the central government (e.g., Ginnie Mae in the US). For Asian social bonds, these issuers include the Korea Student Aid Foundation and Australia's National Housing Finance and Investment Corp.
- Agency–Government Sponsored: A government agency that lacks an explicit government guarantee. The sole example of this among Asian social bond issuers is NongHyup Bank in the Republic of Korea.
- Agency–Government Owned, No Guarantee: A government agency owned fully or partially by the central government but without an explicit guarantee and may have listed equity. For Asian social bonds, this includes the Japan International Cooperation Agency, Industrial Bank of Korea, and Bank of China (Macau).

Figure 7: Total Global Outstanding Social Bonds by United States Dollar Equivalent and Issuer Classification

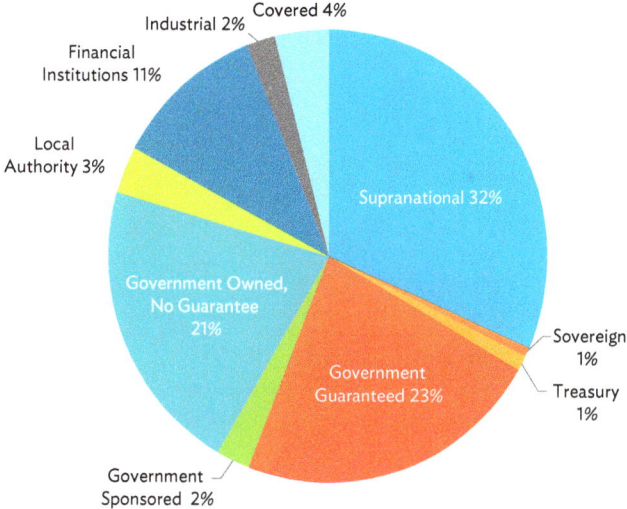

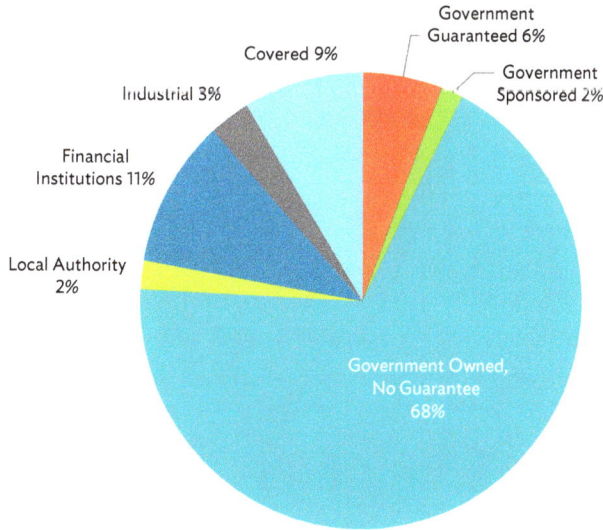

Covered 4%
Industrial 2%
Financial Institutions 11%
Local Authority 3%
Government Owned, No Guarantee 21%
Supranational 32%
Sovereign 1%
Treasury 1%
Government Guaranteed 23%
Government Sponsored 2%

Source: Bloomberg LP.

Figure 8: Total Asian Outstanding Social Bonds by United States Dollar Equivalent and Issuer Classification

Government Guaranteed 6%
Government Sponsored 2%
Covered 9%
Industrial 3%
Financial Institutions 11%
Local Authority 2%
Government Owned, No Guarantee 68%

Source: Bloomberg LP.

Figure 9: Asian Green, Social, and Sustainability Bond Issuance in United States Dollar Equivalent by Year and Issuer Classification

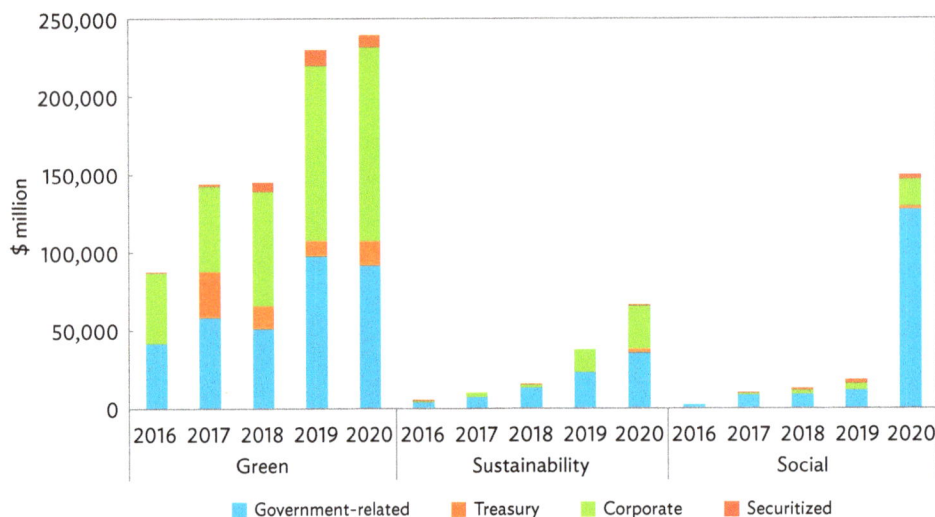

Note: Totals include publicly listed issuances.
Source: Bloomberg LP.

This government-agency-led pattern of issuance reflects the relatively recent emergence of the global social bond market, as government and supranational policy-driven issuers tend to be the first-to-market. They are followed by private financial and industrial issuers, and eventually sovereign and treasury issuers, in response to the broadening awareness and relevance of these instruments. In this sense, the social bond market, globally and in Asia, is following the development path of the larger and more developed green bond market, where corporate issuance has exceeded the combined total of government-related (including supranational issuers) and national treasury issuance since 2018 (Figure 9).

While further growth in corporate social bond issuance would be welcomed by investors eager for higher yields and market diversification, the social bond market will likely continue to have a larger share of government-related issuers whose operating mandates tend to be more aligned with the projects and assets internationally recognized as eligible for social financing.

The breakdown of global outstanding green, sustainability, and social bonds by total notional values (in US dollars) draws this distinction clearly: while nearly 12.3% and 11.3% of outstanding global green bonds were issued by utilities and corporate industrial issuers, respectively, industrial issuers make up only 2.1% of outstanding social bonds, and utility issuance in this sector is nearly zero. On the other hand, covered issuers have been able to carve out a relatively larger share of the social bond market (4.0%) than green bonds (3.0%), with asset-backed securities for the construction of medical facilities and subsidized housing loans for disadvantaged populations leading the way (Figure 10).[24]

---

[24] Covered bonds are securities issued by financial institutions that are secured by dedicated collateral.

Figure 10: Global Outstanding Green, Social, and Sustainability Bonds by Issuer Classification

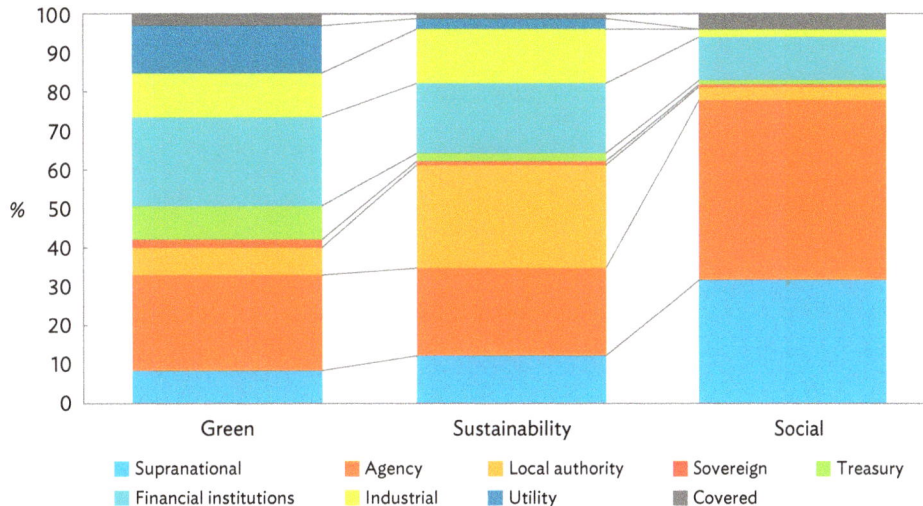

Legend:
- Supranational
- Agency
- Local authority
- Sovereign
- Treasury
- Financial institutions
- Industrial
- Utility
- Covered

Note: Totals include publicly listed issuances.
Source: Bloomberg LP.

Sovereign Social Bond Issuance Grows in Emerging Markets

While much of the social bond market's growth is due to issuances from government agency, supranational, and private financial institutional issuers, local authorities and covered bond issuers of mortgage-backed assets have emerged to add further diversity to the market. The world's first sovereign social bonds were issued in 2020, including Guatemala's $500 million bond to finance COVID-19 response efforts through improved health infrastructure and preventive health practices (Table 6). While technically a supranational and not a sovereign issuer, the European Union in October 2020 issued the world's two largest ever social bonds: EUR10 billion and EUR7 billion bonds with maturities of 10 years and 20 years, respectively. Although not labeled as a social bond and hence not included in our totals, Indonesia also issued a COVID-19 bond with a percentage of proceeds pledged for relief efforts. Also in Asia, with support from ADB, the Government of Thailand issued what appears to have been both the first sovereign pandemic-related and sustainability bond denominated in local currency. In this way, emerging markets in Asia and other regions have demonstrated market leadership by being relatively fast to tap the social bond market for pandemic recovery financing.

Financial Institutions Dominate Private Sector Issuance

Financial institution issuers of social bonds make up the single-largest private sector source of supply in the market, although this share is still small at 16% for the global market and 11% in Asia (excluding supranational issuers). These issuers are typically deposit-taking, private-sector banks, which in Asia include Australian, Japanese, Korean, and Philippine names. Although most social bond issuance in the banking sector in Asia has been in developed market currencies such as US dollars, Australian dollars, and Japanese yen, the Bank of the Philippine Islands issued a PHP-denominated pandemic social bond to fund lending to SMEs. This use of proceeds appears to be well suited for banking sector issuers of social bonds in Asia, with market talk of further large-scale issuance plans for SME financing by other lenders in the region as well.

Table 6: Selected Emerging Market Sovereign ESG Bonds, 2016–2020

Issuer	Ticker	Tenure (years)	Currency	Amount (million)	Type	USD Equivalent (million)
Republic of Poland Government International Bond	POLAND	5.0	EUR	750	Green	780
Fiji Government Bond	FIJIGB	5.0	FJD	50	Green	10
Fiji Government Bond	FIJIGB	13.0	FJD	80	Green	38
Nigeria Government Bond	NIGB	5.0	NGN	10,690	Green	30
Republic of Poland Government International Bond	POLAND	8.5	EUR	1,000	Green	1,227
Perusahaan Penerbit SBSN Indonesia III	INDOIS	5.0	USD	1,250	Green	1,250
Lithuania Government Bond	LITHGB	10.0	EUR	68	Green	82
Perusahaan Penerbit SBSN Indonesia III	INDOIS	5.5	USD	750	Green	750
Republic of Poland Government International Bond	POLAND	30.0	EUR	500	Green	561
Republic of Poland Government International Bond	POLAND	10.0	EUR	1,500	Green	1,684
Hong Kong Government International Bond	HKINTL	5.0	USD	1,000	Green	1,000
Korea International Bond	KOREA	5.0	USD	500	Sustainability	500
Chile Government International Bond	CHILE	30.5	USD	2,318	Green	2,318
Chile Government International Bond	CHILE	12.0	EUR	1,554	Green	1,758
Chile Government International Bond	CHILE	20.0	EUR	1,269	Green	1,397
Ecuador Social Bond Sarl	ECUASO	15.0	USD	327	Social	327
Ecuador Government International Bond	ECUA	15.0	USD	400	Social	400
Guatemala Government Bond	GUATEM	12.0	USD	500	Social	500
Hungary Government International Bond	REPHUN	15.0	EUR	1,500	Green	1,694
Perusahaan Penerbit SBSN Indonesia III	INDOIS	5.0	USD	750	Green	750
Thailand Government Bond	THAIGB	15.3	THB	30,000	Sustainability	966

ESG = environmental, social, and governance; EUR = euro; FJD = Fijian dollar; NGN = Nigerian naira; THB = Thai baht; USD = United States dollar.

Note: Data include both taps and re-openings.

Source: Bloomberg LP.

Nonfinancial corporate issuers make up only a small fraction of the global social bond market (excluding supranational issuers) at 3.0% globally and 2.9% in Asia. This reflects the reality that many social financing activities are seen as the purview of governments and their agencies rather than private sector industrials. It is also apparent that private sector nonfinancial issuers can more readily identify assets and projects for green bonds, which are often physical in nature, than for social assets and projects. Within Asia, the total outstanding stock of nonfinancial corporate green bond issuance is 19.5% from electricity generation, 12.7% from automobiles, and 9.7% from renewable energy, compared with zero issuance from these sectors in the Asian social bond market. So far, the only Asian nonfinancial corporates with social bonds currently outstanding are Japanese companies in the health care and medical devices, educational services, and airlines sectors.

Nonprofit Issuers Emerge in the United States

In another market innovation, the US-based Ford Foundation launched a social bond aimed at ESG investors in June 2020. This was the first such offering by a US nonprofit foundation in the taxable corporate bond market. The bond includes 30-year and 50-year maturities, with $300 million maturing in 2050 at a fixed rate of 2.415% and $700 million maturing in 2070 at a fixed rate of 2.815%. Underscoring the attractiveness of these offerings to mission-oriented investors, the AAA-rated bond was oversubscribed by 5.8 times.[25]

Investors

To a large extent, investor demand has been the driving force behind growth in the social bond market. Consistently and across the globe, investors are increasingly committed to including ESG criteria in their investment decisions. This includes investment in specifically labeled ESG bonds, as well as consideration of ESG risk factors in all investment decisions. In the COVID-19 era, that interest has centered more and more on social bonds that are specifically intended to ease the pain of the pandemic on vulnerable communities worldwide.

A BNP Paribas Asset Management investor survey from June 2020 found that 23% of respondents believe that ESG has become more important as a result of the pandemic. Perhaps most interesting from the survey was the following: "Social issues were considered far more important post- than pre-pandemic; half of respondents saw social issues as important before the crisis, compared with 70% today." Moreover, 79% of respondents "expect social issues to have a positive long-term impact on both investment performance and risk management."[26] This suggests a major increase in sophistication among investors, upending the traditional (and largely disproven) belief that investors must sacrifice financial returns to achieve social goals.

Globally, funds that buy ESG bonds grew by 12% during the first half of 2020, reaching a record $209.5 billion of assets at the end of June according to data from Morningstar. They expect that sustainable fixed-income assets could amount to $260 billion–$280 billion by year-end, fueled by demand from investors for sustainable debt. Alphabet's record $5.75 billion sustainability bond sale in August 2020, for example, was massively oversubscribed with almost $40 billion in orders.[27]

---

[25] *Ford Foundation.* 2020. "Ford Foundation Announces Sale and Pricing of Landmark $1 Billion Social Bonds." 23 June. https://www.fordfoundation.org/the-latest/news/ford-foundation-announces-sale-and-pricing-of-landmark-1-billion-social-bonds/.

[26] A. Basirov, F. Fontan, and A. Gourc. 2020. "2020 Vision: Social Bonds and the S in ESG." *BNP Paribas.* 2 September. https://securities.bnpparibas.com/insights/social-bonds-the-s-in-esg.html.

[27] C. Mutua. 2020. "ESG Bond fund Growth Beats Stocks after COVID-19 Boost." *Financial Planning.* 4 September. https://www.financial-planning.com/articles/coronavirus-pandemic-fuels-sustainable-bond-fund-demand-morningstar.

Investors in ESG bonds may have two reasons to include ESG in their investment management process: the values rationale and the value rationale. Per ADB, the values rationale is "grounded in moral judgment: Individuals are the ultimate owners of most investable assets so they should be invested in ways that make society better off. Not investing in companies that pollute or that produce harmful products creates an incentive for these companies to change their behavior or risk being cut off from investment capital." The value rationale "argues that ESG factors are potential risks to investment portfolios. Integrating ESG analysis into the investment process provides a better assessment of the expected return of an investment and, thus, will generate superior investment returns."[28]

Investors are well aware of the many scandals that have embroiled some businesses—accounting fraud, bribery, money laundering, and environmental disasters—and they choose to avoid these companies for the good of society and the good of their portfolio returns. The ESG approach also improves diversification within portfolios, thus lowering risk while increasing returns.

To these two abovementioned rationales may be added a third: all ESG bonds increase transparency and improve governance. Investors are growing more interested in how their money is used, not only as measured by financial returns but also including social returns, which will increasingly be considered as part of the whole return on investment. The higher levels of transparency and governance associated with ESG bonds help to satisfy the requirement of additionality: these projects are better off being financed by ESG bonds than by straight bonds, and they are therefore more attractive to investors.

In Asia, pension funds and institutional investors largely dominate the investing space. However, in September, Japan's Mitsubishi UFJ issued a JPY150 billion ($1.42 billion) sustainability bond to individual investors for COVID-19 recovery. This made Mitsubishi UFJ the first Asian bank to issue COVID-19 bonds to retail rather than institutional investors, a big step forward in the development of the market.

Other Participants: Philanthropy, Supranationals, and Governments

Philanthropic institutions, supranationals, and governments play an important role in helping to develop the social bond ecosystem and in supporting prospective participants to enter the market. Both supranational institutions and philanthropic institutions have provided invaluable support to the development of the market, from thought leadership to technical assistance to capital guarantees.

Government policymakers and regulators too can play a valuable role in fueling development of the ESG bond market in Asia, as the discussion in Box 2 illustrates.

---

[28] ADB. 2018. *Promoting Green Local Currency Bonds for Infrastructure Development in ASEAN+3.* https://www.adb.org/sites/default/files/publication/410326/green-lcy-bonds-infrastructure-development-asean3.pdf.

Box 2: Examples of Government Enabling Development of the Social Bond Ecosystem

Republic of Korea. In July 2020, the Government of the Republic of Korea announced a "Green Bonds New Deal" to cut carbon emissions and support environmentally friendly industries. This is likely to fuel more interest in environmental, social, and governance debt, as the National Pension Service, which manages $631 billion in assets, plans to boost socially responsible investments, and other investors are likely to follow suit.

Taipei,China. Taipei,China's Securities and Futures Bureau has indicated that social and sustainability bonds could be introduced in Taipei,China by the end of 2020. The Financial Supervisory Commission is actively encouraging companies to raise funds for their environmental and social projects, and to meet their environmental, social, and governance objectives. The Financial Supervisory Commission will ask the Taipei Exchange to establish new guidelines for issuing social and sustainability bonds, which will be slightly different from the current bond guidelines.

Philippines. The Bangko Sentral ng Pilipinas has urged banks to ramp up their social and sustainability bond issuance to help the country recover from the coronavirus disease (COVID-19) pandemic. The central bank has noted that the "health crisis put an enormous brunt on the country's health, educational system, food security, and micro, small, and medium enterprises," adding that banks could channel funds to these sectors to speed up post-pandemic recovery. The Philippines Securities and Exchange Commission has also urged the issuance of social bonds to contain the pandemic, manage its socioeconomic impact, and build resilience to future shocks: "COVID-19 has given rise to serious socioeconomic issues globally, pushing enterprises to the brink of failure and leaving millions of people jobless. The social bond market could boost our response to and recovery from the pandemic by unlocking the much-needed capital for the promotion of public health, reopening of businesses and preservation of jobs, among others." In June 2020, the Securities and Exchange Commission approved the Bank of the Philippine Islands' application to issue COVID-19 Action Response Bonds under the Association of Southeast Asian Nations social bond label.

Sources: K. Cho. 2020. "Korea Overtakes China as Top Asia Sustainable-Debt Seller." *Bloomberg.* 13 August. https://www.bloomberg.com/news/articles/2020-08-13/korea-overtakes-china-as-biggest-sustainable-debt-seller-in-asia; K. Shih-ching. 2020. "Capital Market Forum: Social and Sustainability Bonds Likely by Year's End." *Taipei Times.* 3 August. https://www.taipeitimes.com/News/biz/archives/2020/08/03/2003741027; *Philippines News Agency.* 2020. "SEC Urges Social Bonds to Support Recovery from Pandemic." 30 June. https://www.pna.gov.ph/articles/1107571.

Social Bond Market Characteristics

7

Currency of Issuance

Broken down by currency of issuance, the global social bond market is dominated by EUR-denominated issues, which comprised 68.9% of total outstanding bonds as of the end of 2020. This share is slightly higher than the EUR-denominated share of the green bond market, which is 50.0% (Figure 11). In contrast, the Asian social bond market is more weighted to Japanese yen (7.6%) and other Asian currencies such as the Korean won (4.3%). In the Asian green bond market, the US dollar and Chinese yuan comprise the largest currency shares.

Figure 11: Global Outstanding Green, Sustainability, and Social Bonds by Issuance Currency

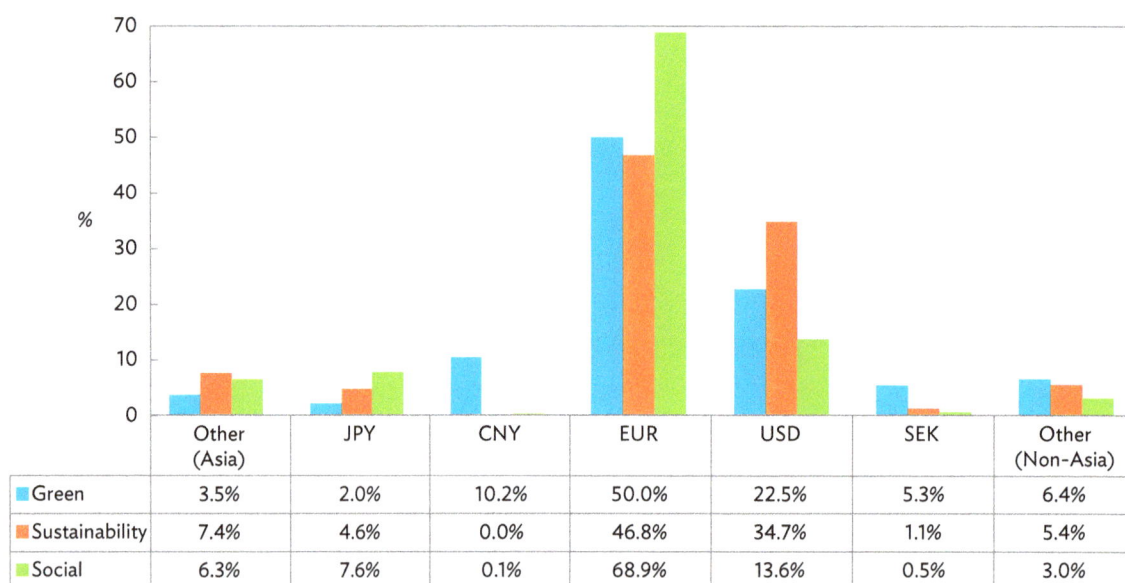

	Other (Asia)	JPY	CNY	EUR	USD	SEK	Other (Non-Asia)
Green	3.5%	2.0%	10.2%	50.0%	22.5%	5.3%	6.4%
Sustainability	7.4%	4.6%	0.0%	46.8%	34.7%	1.1%	5.4%
Social	6.3%	7.6%	0.1%	68.9%	13.6%	0.5%	3.0%

CNY = Chinese yuan, EUR = euro, JPY = Japanese yen, USD = Unite States dollar, SEK= Swedish krona.
Note: Based on sum of notional equivalent.
Source: Bloomberg LP.

Credit Ratings

Broken down by issuer credit rating from international rating agencies, the social bond market almost entirely comprises investment grade (BBB– or better) issues at 99% of total outstanding bonds. The share of investment-grade bonds is similar in the green bond market at 93% (Figure 12). However, the social bond market shows an even higher concentration of the prime AAA and AA sectors at 79% of the market, compared with 37% for green bonds, reflecting the social bond market's higher share of government agency and supranational bond issuance. Accordingly, we estimate that the weighted average credit rating of the global social bond market is AA, compared with a weighted average of A+ in the global green bond market and AA– in the global sustainability bond market.

Figure 12: Global Outstanding Green, Sustainability, and Social Bonds by Credit Rating

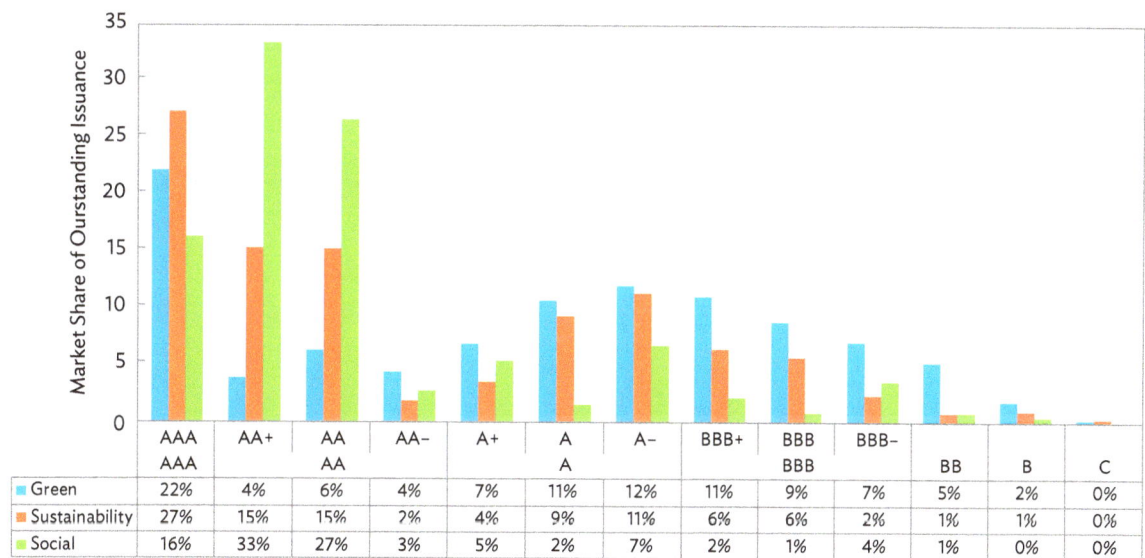

	AAA AAA	AA+	AA AA	AA–	A+	A A	A–	BBB+	BBB BBB	BBB–	BB	B	C
Green	22%	4%	6%	4%	7%	11%	12%	11%	9%	7%	5%	2%	0%
Sustainability	27%	15%	15%	2%	4%	9%	11%	6%	6%	2%	1%	1%	0%
Social	16%	33%	27%	3%	5%	2%	7%	2%	1%	4%	1%	0%	0%

Note: Based on sum of notional equivalent.
Source: Bloomberg LP.

Size of Issuance

Broken down by issuance size, it is apparent that the global ESG bond market no longer entirely comprises small-sized individual bonds, as individual debt sales of $500 million or more are no longer headline events. Still, only 40% of total outstanding global social bonds have a notional value of $250 million or more, versus 33% for green bonds, representing limited liquidity conditions for many smaller ESG bond issues (Figure 13). Large social bond offerings are becoming more common, however, with 12% of outstanding social bond issues sized $1 billion or more. We estimate that the average issue size of current outstanding social bonds globally is $540 million, including recent jumbo issuances, compared with $300 million for green bonds and $450 million for sustainability bonds.

Figure 13: Global Outstanding Green, Sustainability, and Social Bonds by United States Dollar Equivalent Issuance Size

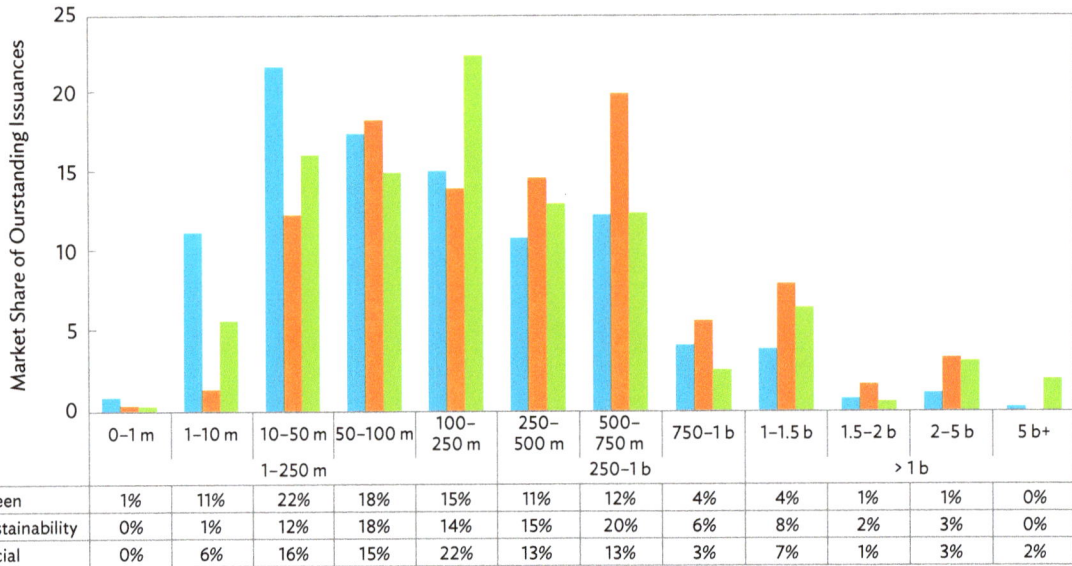

	0–1 m	1–10 m	10–50 m	50–100 m	100–250 m	250–500 m	500–750 m	750–1 b	1–1.5 b	1.5–2 b	2–5 b	5 b+
			1–250 m				250–1 b			> 1 b		
■ Green	1%	11%	22%	18%	15%	11%	12%	4%	4%	1%	1%	0%
■ Sustainability	0%	1%	12%	18%	14%	15%	20%	6%	8%	2%	3%	0%
■ Social	0%	6%	16%	15%	22%	13%	13%	3%	7%	1%	3%	2%

(Market Share of Outstanding Issuances, vertical axis 0–25)

b = billion, m = million.
Source: Bloomberg LP.

8

Asian Social Bond Market Characteristics

Issuers from Japan and the Republic of Korea Dominate

A survey of the major Asian social bond issuers of at least $100 million equivalent shows a concentration of issuers in government-related sectors in Japan and the Republic of Korea, as well as private sector financial issuers (Table 7). The largest Asian social bond issuer by far is East Nippon Expressway Co. Ltd., which operates express toll roads in the eastern half of Japan's main island of Honshu and has developed a social bond framework organized around issues including regional revitalization, disaster preparedness and response, and traffic safety (Box 3). Government agency issuers in the Republic of Korea include the Korea SME and Startups Agency, Korea Housing Finance Corporation, and the Industrial Bank of Korea, which have also come to be relatively active issuers in the Asian social bond market with issuances in US dollars, euros, and Korean won.

Table 7: Outstanding Social Bond Issuances in Asia—$100 Million Equivalent or More

	Equivalent ($ million)
AUSTRALIA	**1,203**
Corporate	**381**
National Australia Bank Ltd.	381
Government-Related	**822**
National Housing Finance and Investment Corp.	822
PEOPLE'S REPUBLIC OF CHINA	**857**
Government-Related	**857**
Bank of China Ltd. (Macau)	640
Beijing Infrastructure Investment Co. Ltd.	218
INDIA	**500**
Corporate	**500**
Shriram Transport Finance Co. Ltd.	500
JAPAN	**11,159**
Corporate	**663**
University of Tokyo National University Corp.	190
Nipro Corp.	474
Government-Related	**10,495**
East Nippon Expressway Co. Ltd.	4,809
Hanshin Expressway Co. Ltd.	1,071
Japan International Cooperation Agency	1,660
Japan Student Services Organization	2,764
Urban Renaissance Agency	192

continued on next page

Table 7   *continued*

	Equivalent ($ million)
PHILIPPINES	**438**
Corporate	**438**
Bank of the Philippine Islands	438
REPUBLIC OF KOREA	**12,834**
Corporate	**1,185**
Shinhan Bank Co. Ltd.	285
Shinhan Card Co. Ltd.	400
Shinhan Financial Group Co. Ltd.	500
Government-Related	**8,858**
Export–Import Bank of Korea	587
Industrial Bank of Korea	1,000
KDIC Special Account Bond	737
Korea Development Bank	1,269
Korea Hydro & Nuclear Power Co. Ltd.	220
Korea Land & Housing Corp.	500
Korea SMEs and Startups Agency	3,934
Korea Student Aid Foundation	110
NongHyup Bank	500
Securitized	**2,792**
Korea Housing Finance Corp.	2,792
Grand Total	**26,991**

Source: Bloomberg LP.

Box 3: Social Bond Case Study—East Nippon Expressway

Launched in June 2019, East Nippon Expressway's social bond series is being used to fund affordable basic infrastructure in three categories:

- construct new and reconstruct existing expressways to promote development of cities and communities by encouraging investment in regional industries and tourism;
- repair expressways and enable recovery from disasters to mitigate risks from mega-earthquakes and tsunamis, improve traffic safety, and promote environmental conservation; and
- address aging infrastructure.

The bond's target investor population is the general public, and the series of offerings aimed to advance progress on a number of the United Nations Sustainable Development Goals. Notably, the bond series received a third-party evaluation of its social objectives that confirms its alignment with the Social Bond Principles.

Source: *R&I Social Bond Opinions.* 2019. "East Nippon Expressway Co., Ltd. (NEXCO East) Social Finance Framework." 4 June. https://www.r-i.co.jp/en/opinion_social/2019/06/opinion_social_20190604_eng.pdf.

ICMA–Compliant Social Bonds Are Rare in the People's Republic of China

Social bond issuance in the PRC that adheres to internationally recognized standards, such as the ICMA guidelines, has so far been extremely limited (Figure 14). This partly reflects the early emergence of the PRC's onshore COVID-19 bonds based on a local market structure not generally recognized by international investors. However, the contrast with the degree of the PRC's dominance in the Asian green bond market remains stark (Figure 15).

Figure 14: Asian Social Bond Issuance by Economy of Origin

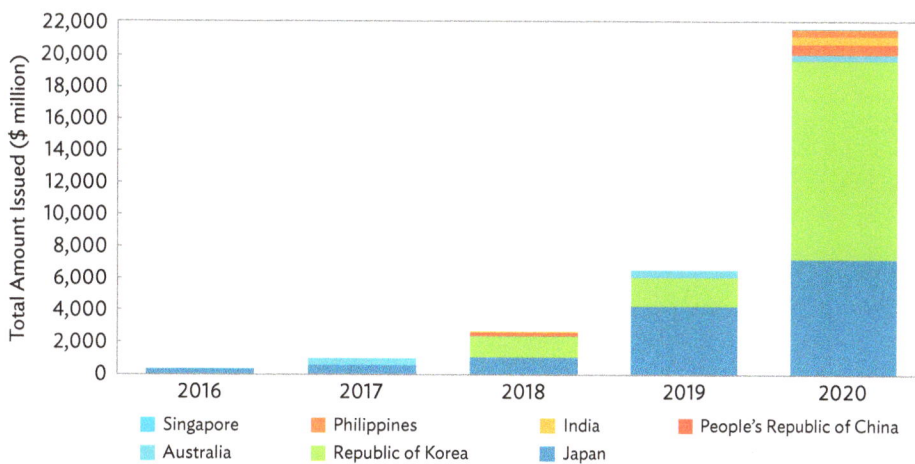

Legend: Singapore, Philippines, India, People's Republic of China, Australia, Republic of Korea, Japan

Source: Bloomberg LP.

Figure 15: Market Shares of Asian Green, Sustainability, and Social Bonds Outstanding by Economy of Origin

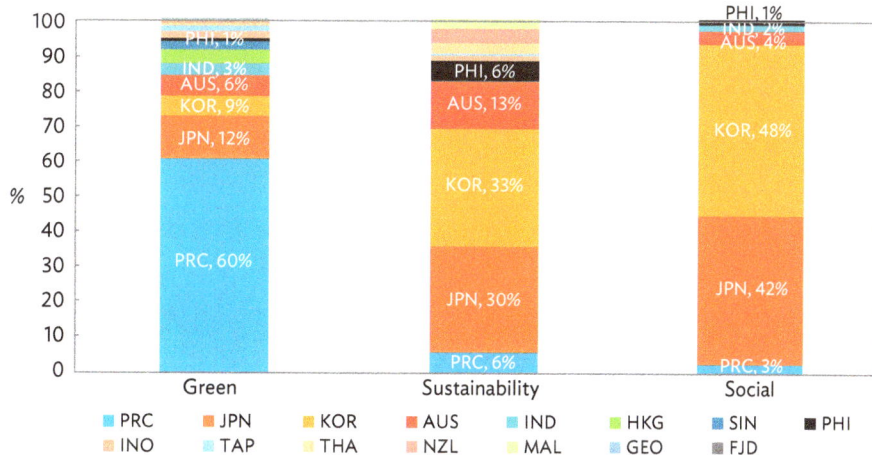

Green: PHI, 1%; IND, 3%; AUS, 6%; KOR, 9%; JPN, 12%; PRC, 60%

Sustainability: PHI, 6%; AUS, 13%; KOR, 33%; JPN, 30%; PRC, 6%

Social: PHI, 1%; IND, 2%; AUS, 4%; KOR, 48%; JPN, 42%; PRC, 3%

Legend: PRC, JPN, KOR, AUS, IND, HKG, SIN, PHI, INO, TAP, THA, NZL, MAL, GEO, FJD

AUS = Australia; FIJ = Fiji; GEO = Georgia; HKG = Hong Kong, China; IND = India; INO = Indonesia; JPN = Japan; KOR = Republic of Korea; MAL = Malaysia; NZL = New Zealand; PHI = Philippines; PRC = People's Republic of China; SIN = Singapore; TAP = Taipei,China; THA = Thailand.
Source: Bloomberg LP.

Many First-Time Issuers in 2020

Many of the Asian social bond issuers in 2020 were entirely new entrants to the ESG bond market. For example, the Government of Thailand issued its first local-currency-denominated sustainability bond in August, which was also the sovereign's first ESG bond. Shriram Transport Finance Company, a non-bank financial institution based in Mumbai, also issued its first social bond in 2020 (Box 4). This suggests that social and sustainability bond issuance is deepening and diversifying the Asian ESG bond market in important ways.

Box 4: Social Bond Case Study—Shriram Transport Finance Company

Shriram, a non-bank financial institution based in Mumbai, issued its first social bond in 2020 to support microfinance and employment generation via funding for small and medium-sized enterprises.

The use of proceeds for Shriram's social bond issuance includes the provision of

- financing for small road transport operators and first-time buyers from underserved communities at favorable interest rates, excluding vehicles that are used in environmentally unfriendly industries such as coal;
- financial instruments and support for micro, small, and medium-sized industries in India; and
- affordable loans to support entrepreneurs from low-income Indian states.

This social bond was the issuer's first environmental, social, and governance (ESG) bond. It is aligned with United Nations Sustainable Development Goal Number 8 (decent work and economic growth) and Number 10 (reduced inequalities). It was reviewed by KPMG and Sustainalytics, which reported that the project is "credible and impactful, and aligns with the four core components of the Social Bond Principles 2018."

Source: *Sustainalytics Second-Party Opinion*. 2020. "Shriram Social Bond Framework." January. https://cdn.stfc.in/stfc/uploads/2020/01/STFC_Sustainalytics-Second-Party-Opinion.pdf.

Among sovereigns, Indonesia issued $4.3 billion in COVID-19 response bonds, with maturities of 10, 30, and 50 years. While this issue had many features of a social bond, it was not compliant with the SBP, in part due to the contrast between its long tenure versus the much shorter duration of projects to be funded by the bond.[29] The due diligence required to comply with these principles can take too long for developing economies in urgent need of fresh funding.

Asian Issuers Still Heavily Concentrated in High-Income Economies

As this paper's analysis of the Asian social bond universe demonstrates, issuances so far have been dominated by government-related agency issuers in high-income economies such as Japan and the Republic of Korea, where such agency issuance comprises 37% and 34% of the social bond market in these countries, respectively. Furthermore, social bond issuance from government agencies tends to be concentrated in a small number of issuers, typically policy lending banks and sovereign agencies with a clear social function such as housing corporations, SME lending, and student aid foundations. In terms of currency denomination,

---

[29] J. Rogers. 2020. "Asia's SSAs Fall Short as Social Bonds Hit the COVID-19 Agenda." *The Asset.* 5 June. https://www.theasset.com/covid-19/40719/asias-ssas-fall-short-as-social-bonds-hit-the-covid-19-agenda-.

these government-agency social bonds tend to be denominated in the local currency of their respective issuing economy, although 28% of agency social bonds in the Republic of Korea are issued in US dollars or euro rather than Korean won, and they are issued primarily by policy banks. As such, the main investors for such issues are likely to be domestic buy-and-hold asset owners.

The pandemic-precipitated rise of the social bond sector is both a challenge and an opportunity, especially with regard to heightened demands for transparent and reliable measurements of social impact. A Bloomberg report predicts that "…social bond reporting and disclosure practices will gain importance particularly as concerns around "social washing"—when an issuer misrepresents the social impact of its financed projects— grow in the investor community given the challenges of tracking the impact of social bonds. This challenge is compounded by the fact that benefits are often more qualitative than quantitative." While the updated ICMA recommendations will probably help in this regard, market demand for transparency may outstrip improvements in reporting and transparency for some time to come.[30]

Nonetheless, it also seems likely that both investors' and issuers' attraction to social bonds will not fade with the eventual end of the COVID-19 crisis. Many participants suggest that, in the past, the market was limited by a lack of clear definitions and targets. But now, the pandemic has imbued the social bond market with a much more focused vision on these issues, particularly with regard to concrete goals and metrics to assess progress toward those goals.

[30] Footnote 14.

Overcoming Obstacles to Social Bond Market Growth in Asia

9

While the need for social bond market growth is obvious and imperative, there are significant obstacles to market growth that must be addressed. It is generally agreed that the greatest obstacles to growth in the social bond space are the lack of clarity about measuring and assessing impact, as well as a supply-side shortage. More precisely, there has not yet been a coalescing around standardization in the measurement of impact, which is extremely difficult to do because social bond projects and assets are by their very nature much more diverse than green bond projects and assets. While the ICMA framework is a step forward, it falls well short of a standardized set of metrics that would enable comparison of impact performance across instruments. Surveys find that asset owners and managers view social impact as the most difficult sector to analyze—compared with, for example, environmental impact; hence, finding solutions to this issue would vastly open up the field.[31]

Without this clarity, the risk of social washing, or overstating the social value of a bond, is very real, and investors are keenly aware of this risk. Indeed, even before the emergence of COVID-19 bonds, many market participants worried about "rainbow bonds" in which all matter of labels might go hand in hand with greenwashing or social washing.

Some research also suggests that the need for higher issuance volume and diversity (i.e., more corporate issuers) is another significant obstacle to market growth. A targeted investor survey found that organizations without a dedicated social bond fund cited insufficient issuance volumes, lack of issuer diversity, no demand from clients, and lack of indices for benchmarking as their most important reasons for not creating such a fund.[32]

This is a bit of a vicious cycle. Mainstream investors (i.e., those who do not have a strong preference for ESG-linked investing) do not really understand the purpose and value of social bonds. This limits investor demand to niche status, which has then discouraged more widespread issuance and market development, thereby making it harder to explain what social bonds are for.

But the advent of COVID-19 brings an opportunity to turn this into a virtuous cycle, as attention is high and focused, and the need for financing is immense.

Financial advisors, in particular, may be an obstacle to market growth, as they are often poorly informed on this sector and may believe that ESG investments detract from returns. They may also think that ESG applies largely to the equity sector; therefore, they may be resistant to driving their clients into socially responsible, fixed-income investments.

Also, many Asian sovereigns and corporates that would like to participate in the social bond market—and probably will in the future—do not yet have social bond frameworks in place. It takes time, money, and

---

[31] Footnote 17.
[32] ICMA. 2020. *GBP/SBP Social Bonds Working Group Survey March–April.* https://www.icmagroup.org/assets/documents/Regulatory/Green-Bonds/SummarySurvey-SBWG-2020-Results-190520.pdf.

human resources to develop ICMA-compliant issuance procedures, all of which may be limited resources in some parts of developing Asia. The due diligence required to become ICMA-compliant is significant and thus an obstacle to participation in this market. Sovereigns and corporates alike often have to get departments and ministries that are typically siloed from each other to join together, which is a challenge; but once achieved, it can result in better long-term collaboration.

Issuing an ESG bond, which requires an ESG bond framework and second-party opinion, also typically requires the issuer to obtain an ESG evaluation by the second party, which takes time and preparation. This gives issuers a good reason to pre-commit to ESG so as to be ready when the crisis comes; the firms that did the ESG work ahead of time have been able to come to market faster.

Of course, with every challenge comes an opportunity, and there is certainly a broad opportunity for market participants to develop this holy grail: a widely accepted, standardized set of metrics to assess social impact. Various bodies—from the Sustainability Accounting Standards Board to European authorities—are pursuing a system of standardized reporting to include social impact. There is, however, a continuing debate in the market between the right mix of regulatory oversight versus market-principles-based oversight.

Fortunately, noninvestment actors—including philanthropic foundations, multilateral institutions, and financial institutions—can help to overcome these obstacles, mitigate these risks, and continue to build on the momentum of 2020 in the social bond market. It is crucial that an ecosystem comes into existence, especially in Asia, to support and educate potential market participants.

Philanthropic and Multilateral Organizations

Given the very limited amount of money that philanthropy can bring to the table relative to the huge funding gap, it may seem at first that this sector has a limited role to play in building the social bond market. This first impression, however, is far from the reality; in fact, philanthropy can have a major catalytic role in the development of a robust social bond market in Asia. For example, donors can support social financing by providing concessional working capital loans and guarantees of principal to help reduce the risks and costs of social bonds for both the issuer and investor.

Perhaps even more important than money, however, is the expertise and the halo effect of philanthropy in building this market. Philanthropic organizations can serve as thought leaders, providing market research and education, particularly for investors and financial advisors. They can support the development of industry standards and guidelines that will help reduce the risk of social washing. They can provide technical assistance to sovereign issuers, especially around the knotty issue of impact measurement. And by acting as seed investors, foundations can convey a halo effect that will reassure and crowd in investors.

Multilateral institutions can play a similar role to that of philanthropic organizations with regard to market-building. ADB, for example, assisted the Government of Thailand in designing, issuing, and monitoring innovative capital market initiatives as part of the country's recovery from the COVID-19 pandemic. ADB's technical assistance through the ASEAN Catalytic Green Finance Facility includes bond framework development and external reviews to help Thailand's Ministry of Finance and National Housing Authority design green, social, and sustainability bonds in accordance with global and ASEAN standards.[33]

---

[33] C. Santiago. 2020. "ADB Supports Thailand Green Bonds for COVID-10 Recovery." *The Asset.com*. https://www.theasset.com/article-esg/41811/adb-supports-thailand-green-bonds-for-covid-19-recovery.

Multilateral development banks worldwide will need to support private investors through advisory services and advocacy for policy reform. Market education, such as case studies and data dissemination, is important. These institutions may need to step up and assume the riskiest parts of private sector investments, especially in the early stages of the deals, in order to urge private capital into the poorest, riskiest countries.

Governments

It is possible that emerging market sovereigns simply have not had enough time to create ICMA-compliant social bond frameworks amid the urgency of the need for funds to combat COVID-19 and its fallout.[34] The process to set this up at the sovereign level, which may include overcoming silo issues among various government ministries and finding the applicable assets, is cumbersome. Accordingly, these process issues are a major factor holding back labeled sovereign issuance, even in the best of times. This suggests that sovereign issuers should consider setting up a social bond framework preemptively to speed the issuance process in times of general crisis such as the COVID-19 pandemic and potential future disasters.

Governments in developing Asia as well as the developed world have a critical role to play in raising funds to meet social and environmental challenges. To address the gaping educational deficit outlined above and in support of SDG Number 4 (high-quality education), the governments of the United Kingdom, Norway, the Netherlands, Denmark, and Sweden have pledged to help guarantee and reduce the cost of new bonds to provide low-cost loans for education in lower-middle-income economies.

The International Finance Facility for Education, launched in 2020, aims to galvanize at least $10 billion in bonds issued by multilateral development banks. This facility is a model for how developed country governments can work together to support the crowding in of public and private sector investment in education and other social areas. Through both grants and guarantees, these efforts can lower borrowing costs and risks, thus providing benefits for issuers and investors alike.

Governments in developing Asia need to provide a conducive regulatory and institutional framework to support the growth of the social bond market. Just as important, a signal in the form of government issuance of ESG bonds can do a lot to catalyze more corporate issuance. It sets a precedent and lends more legitimacy when potential market participants see that the government itself is participating in the market.

Judging from the earlier development of the green bond market, sovereign ESG bond issuance has tended to lag rather than lead the emergence and development of domestic ESG bond markets, although this is mainly an observation from developed European markets. Regarding the necessity of building a "green yield curve" or a "social yield curve," while some European sovereign issuers like Germany have taken steps to develop such markets, the absence of such curves is not likely to be a factor in the early stage of market development.

This is because ESG bonds tend to trade closely with their conventional bond counterparts as mainstream investors are generally unwilling to pay more for an ESG label on pari passu assets. In fact, an ESG premium on such issuance, while no doubt attractive to bond issuers and possibly capable of incentivizing new supply, would likely be offset by the corresponding reduction of investment attractiveness for bond buyers. Rather, several countries including Japan have established subsidy programs to offset the additional costs to issuers of preparing green or social bond frameworks such as consulting and ratings expenses.

---

[34] Footnote 33.

As investors are wary of excessive fragmentation in the global social bond market, it is preferable that when it is necessary for domestic social bond frameworks to reflect national circumstances or laws and customs, they be developed to be aligned with global standards such as ICMA to the extent possible. Where appropriate, major government pension funds may consider public commitments to invest in ESG bonds, including social bonds, as a means of signaling to private institutional investors and issuers.

On the private sector side, governments can work to raise awareness, especially via the banking sector and other financial intermediaries, of the social bond concept and how it may be more suited to certain industries and issuer types who wish to tap into the growing trend for ESG investments but who are not as naturally aligned to green or climate goals. Finally, while the need to maintain consistent and science-based green bond definitions and taxonomies has caused considerable back and forth in the green finance arena, it may be that the more qualitative nature of social bond impacts need not be as fractious, thereby making the projects they finance easier to implement as long as sufficient investor demand can be developed.

The main takeaway for policy makers of less-advanced economies in Asia who are looking to grow their own domestic social bond market may be to establish a social bond issuance program at a flagship government agency with a focused mandate on social-financing-aligned sectors (e.g., housing, SME lending, or student aid). Alternatively, governments may encourage policy banks to issue social bonds in local or external currencies to give both local and foreign investors access to social financing opportunities through more internationally recognized issuers.

Islamic Finance

Another opportunity to expand the social bond market is to increase the contribution of Islamic financing to ESG-linked funding. Social finance is a natural adjunct to Islamic finance, given the latter's adherence to religious principles and social welfare. Islamic finance is also an important growth area in parts of developing Asia. Malaysia, for example, accounts for more than 25% of the global Islamic banking market; over 90% of Muslims in that country engage in *zakat*, which is an obligatory payment made annually under Islamic law to be used for charitable and religious purposes. Indonesia is home to the world's largest Muslim population at more than 230 million people, or 88% of the country's total population. Previous Indonesian green sovereign bonds have been issued in the *wakalah sukuk* format, which in Indonesia includes an allocation register framework for tagging a pool of compliant projects and assets, and for managing cash flows. So in this case, Sharia-compliant *sukuk* are ready-made for green bonds and social finance according to ICMA principles.

The governments of these countries are waking up to the potential for Islamic finance to achieve social goals. In June 2020, Indonesia raised $2.5 billion from a three-tranche global *sukuk* intended to help the government fund the battle against COVID-19. The issue was oversubscribed at 6.7 times its target, reflecting strong investor interest in these instruments. Its success demonstrates the viability of the Islamic finance sector in raising funds to alleviate social ills, particularly in the era of COVID-19; it also illustrates the potential for developing social-bond-like instruments in the Islamic finance market.

Gender Lens Investing

Gender lens investing is an approach to investing that seeks the social and economic empowerment of women, alongside financial returns. A gender-lens-investing approach enables investors to channel funds to businesses that create positive gender outcomes, such as supporting women entrepreneurs, developing products and services that benefit women, and funding businesses with a high share of female executives. In the COVID-19 context, this could potentially be applied to finance for women entrepreneurs or childcare, for example.

One such financial instrument is the IIX Women's Livelihood Bond series, which won the UN Global Climate Action Award in 2019. While relatively small at around $150 million, this series seeks to create sustainable livelihoods for over 2 million women in Asia. It specifically links women to climate change, both with regard to their vulnerability and their ability to act as agents of change. The bond series, which was three times oversubscribed, can be listed on both social and traditional stock exchanges.

The Way Forward

10

There is undoubtedly an urgent and compelling case for the development of a robust social bond market in Asia. Harnessing the power of private capital to address critical social needs is an opportunity for both issuers and investors to address these needs in a financial context. While the pandemic will fade away, one lasting impact may well be its catalytic effect on the development of social bond markets worldwide. Much as the beautifully clear skies and air during the stringent lockdowns of early 2020 illustrated the environmental damage being wrought by business and industry, the pandemic has also highlighted the peril of ignoring social risks in our investment decisions. In Asia, a June 2020 survey by the Investment Management Association of Singapore found that 66% of respondents believe that COVID-19 will accelerate the adoption of ESG investments.[35]

Even before the pandemic hit, a report by the Business and Sustainable Development Commission estimated that achieving the SDGs could open up $12 trillion of market opportunities in food and agriculture, cities, energy and materials, and health and well-being, while also creating 380 million new jobs by 2030.

So we know that achieving the SDGs makes business sense.[36] This means that financial instruments aimed at pursuing social as well as financial value can play a critical role in fostering growth and progress in developing Asia.

Interest in investing in bonds that pursue ESG goals alongside financial returns was already mounting before the onset of the COVID-19 pandemic. However, much of this interest focused on instruments that addressed climate change and environmental concerns, while social bonds lagged well behind. Then the pandemic refocused both issuers and investors on the urgent need for innovative financial instruments such as social bonds to address the social challenges that have become so much more pressing in the era of COVID-19. A Bloomberg report commented: "Recent events around the world have… highlighted the necessity for societies and companies to invest in social justice and social resilience permanently, rather than temporarily in response to the pandemic."[37]

An overly narrow focus on COVID-19-specific issues for social bond issuers, of course, will eventually be a dead end. So how should issuers and investors leverage the increased market awareness of social factors for sustainability projects beyond climate change? Every actor in the ecosystem has a role to play. Governments, supranationals, and philanthropic institutions can all support the development of this market, offering technical assistance, guarantees of capital, education, thought leadership, and a supportive regulatory environment. Issuers can seek out social investment opportunities and put into place the scaffolding for social bond issues that can be quickly erected and completed in accordance with ICMA and ASEAN guidelines. And investors,

---

[35] *The Asset.* 2020. "COVID-19 to Accelerate ESG Adoption in Investment Industry." 14 August. https://www.theasset.com/article-esg/41295/covid-19-to-accelerate-esg-adoption-in-investment-industry.

[36] N. Vali. 2017. "More than Philanthropy: SDGs Are a $12 Trillion Opportunity for the Private Sector." *UNDP.* 25 August. https://www.undp.org/content/undp/en/home/blog/2017/8/25/More-than-philanthropy-SDGs-present-an-estimated-US-12-trillion-in-market-opportunities-for-private-sector-through-inclusive-business.html.

[37] *BloombergNEF Sustainability Team.* 2020. "COVID-19 Indicators: Sustainability." 6 August.

who are the key to making this work, should seek out well-constructed and well-documented social bond investments while remaining ever vigilant for social washing.

The overall ESG bond market is still small at about 5% of the total global bond market. But the pandemic has proven the concept and value of social bonds to address social challenges and achieve the SDGs. This provides a solid basis for the market to continue its path toward maturity in the post-pandemic environment.

Social bonds have emerged as the premier fixed-income instrument for addressing the social and economic fallout from COVID-19. They may be used to fund employment generation projects, medical equipment manufacturing, social services, and more—all of which mitigate the worst effects of the pandemic on marginalized populations. Asia, however, has lagged behind other parts of the world, issuing only a handful of ICMA-compliant social bonds to date.

This is a call to action for Asia to rapidly ramp up its participation in the social bond market. The use of ICMA- or ASEAN-compliant social bonds is an opportunity for Asia to capitalize on fast-growing investor demand for these instruments, while raising funds to alleviate the damage wrought by COVID-19. Further, it is an opportunity to use these innovative financial instruments to direct private capital at scale to address long-standing social ills even as the pandemic eases and a new global normal emerges.

www.ingramcontent.com/pod-product-compliance
Lightning Source LLC
Chambersburg PA
CBHW042035220326

41599CB00045BA/7403